Paragraph Power

Also from Prentice Hall Regents by George M. Rooks:

Share Your Paragraph: An Interactive Approach to Writing
2nd Edition

PARAGRAPH
2nd Edition

POWER

Communicating
Ideas Through
Paragraphs

For Upper Intermediate Students of English

GEORGE M. ROOKS

UNIVERSITY OF CALIFORNIA, DAVIS

Pearson Education, 10 Bank Street, White Plains, NY 10606

Rooks, George.
    Paragraph power : communicating ideas through paragraphs / George
M. Rooks. -- 2nd ed.
        p. cm.
    "For upper intermediate students of English."
    ISBN 0-13-660754-3
    1. English language--Paragraphs--Problems, exercises, etc.
    2. English language--Textbooks for foreign speakers.   I. Title.
    PE1439.R65   1999
    808'.042--dc21   98-31833
                                                        CIP

Publisher: *Mary Jane Peluso*
Acquisitions Editor: *Sheryl Olinsky*
AVP/Director of Production and Manufacturing: *Aliza Greenblatt*
Executive Managing Editor: *Dominick Mosco*
Development, Interior Design,
    Electronic Production: *Noël Vreeland Carter*
Manufacturing Manager: *Ray Keating*
Art Director: *Merle Krumper*
Cover Design: *Susan Newman Design Inc.*
Electronic Publishing Specialist: *Steven D. Greydanus*
Photo Research: *Noël Vreeland Carter*

Photo and Art Credits:
Chapter 1: Page 3, Hawaii Tourism Office, Page 17, Michelle LoGerfo, Page 21, Michal Heron/Simon & Schuster/PH College, Page 22, Israel Government Tourist Office; *Chapter 2:* Page 46 (left) Library of Congress, (right) Michal Heron, Page 47, Randy Taylor/Sygma; *Chapter 3:* Page 68, Courtesy Dr. Michael Hadfield, Department of Zoology, University of Hawaii/Photo by Frank LaBua, Page 69, Michelle LoGerfo; *Chapter 4:* Page 89, Lorena E. Cerisano, Page 90, Karen Holland; *Chapter 5:* Page 115, NASA Headquarters; *Chapter 6:* Page 139, (left) Noël Vreeland Carter, (right) Dit Mosco; *Chapter 8:* Page 172, Natalie Anderson, Page 178, Michal Heron/Simon & Schuster/PH College.

Printed in the United States of America
10 9 8 7 6 5 4 3

0-13-660754-3

To Hila, for her inspiration and support

Contents

Appendix A: Grammar Practice 181

Appendix B: Checklist for Students and Teachers 203

What's New in This Edition

More than ten years have passed since the first edition of *Paragraph Power* appeared. The author would like to thank the many teachers and students who have commented on the strengths of the text and suggested ways to improve it.

In this new edition, the author has attempted to incorporate as many of those suggestions as possible in addition to the usual updating of information contained in the text. The text has been enlivened by the addition of communicative exercises as well as many new model paragraphs.

More important, this new edition reflects a shift away from the totally "nonpersonal" writing emphasized in the first edition. Some teachers have suggested that university writing sometimes does include writing of a personal nature. Thus there are now model paragraphs using "I" in this edition.

Once again, thanks to all who have used and enjoyed this text over the years.

George Rooks
University of California, Davis

Paragraph Power is designed for an upper-intermediate-level writing class in an English as a Second Language (ESL) program. The contents provide activities sufficient (at least) for a daily class of quarter length (ten weeks). Students entering the class should have a basic grounding in grammar and should be able to write clear sentences.

Paragraph Power is based on the following ideas:

1. Many ESL students are attempting to enter a university in the United States. Therefore, this book emphasizes nonpersonal writing of the type expected in universities. The topics for writing in each chapter are merely suggestions; students should be encouraged to choose topics relevant to their field of study.

2. Some composition books are explanation-heavy. Students are supposed to learn by reading through explanations rather than by communication activities. This is, conversely, a book designed to stimulate students' ideas about writing and to teach them how to communicate their ideas more clearly and effectively.

3. A key means of improving writing is through careful reading. Therefore, students are frequently asked to analyze sentences containing grammatical mistakes, and sentences with organizational and developmental weaknesses. Each student is taught to criticize other writers' sentences and paragraphs, and is encouraged to criticize his or her own sentences and paragraphs before submitting his or her writing to the teacher.

4. Flexibility is crucial. The teacher must pace and supplement as appropriate. The book is designed for a ten-week program, but with some supplemental activities, it might well be suitable for a fourteen-week schedule. Under other circumstances, it might be useful as a six- or seven-week program.

OVERVIEW OF MATERIAL

The first two chapters instill in the student ideas of what a paragraph is and what its parts are. At the end of each of these chapters, students are asked to write a paragraph using examples, details, or factual information.

Chapters 3 through 7 focus on five specific rhetorical forms: description, process, cause and effect, comparison and contrast, and argument. These are arranged in ascending order of difficulty. Students are directed to produce one paragraph in each form.

By the time the student reaches Chapter 8, it is assumed that he or she will have a firm grasp of basic paragraph structure. Accordingly, the remaining rhetorical forms of definition, cause and effect, classification, natural process, and neutral argument are presented in the form of model paragraphs accompanied by concise explanations. A sample inductive paragraph is then included as an example of organizational variety.

Appendix A contains a series of grammatical exercises to be completed individually or collectively (as needed) by the student or class.

Appendix B contains a checklist for the student to use before submitting his or her paragraph, and for the teacher to use as a guide in evaluation.

SUGGESTED COURSE OUTLINE

It is suggested that each class spend a minimum of five hours on Chapter 1 (conceptual), nine hours on Chapter 7 (the most complex), and seven hours on each of Chapters 2 through 6. This latter time might be apportioned as follows:

four or five hours covering textual material,

one hour producing the paragraph,

one hour reviewing aspects of student writing in class,

one hour incorporating teacher's suggestions into a final revision.

Covering textual material

The largest portion of in-class textual time should be spent discussing and analyzing the paragraphs in the text and completing the accompanying activities. Clearly, a variety of presentations is essential if students are to be stimulated. One effective technique is to have students complete the analyses and activities individually; then group or pair the students and have them compare their answers collectively; and finally, bring the class together and discuss the answers as a class.

It is a strongly recommended that the teacher (or students) bring to class supplemental paragraphs from other sources to illustrate textual concepts. Supplemental material may also be desirable when discussing grammatical points, such as passive voice (Chapter 3) and relative clauses (Chapter 6). Appendix A contains grammar and stylistic exercises that may be approached individually (for example, if some students have continuing problems with fragments, they may be asked to do exercises 3 and 4) or as a class if the teacher feels this is appropriate.

Writing the paragraph

It is important for students to write their paragraphs in class with a certain time limit in order to acclimate themselves to the pressures they will face in university courses.

From the outset, the dynamic process of planning, writing, in-writing revision, rough draft revision, and final editing should be emphasized. On the day paragraphs are written, students should be reminded to spend time planning and revising. The editing process should include the completion of the Checklist for Students and Teachers (Appendix B). The checklist is an important tool that students can use for self-improvement and that the teacher can use for consistent evaluation.

Each chapter contains multiple suggestions for writing (factual and imaginative), but students should be free to choose other topics if they are so motivated, and if they discuss them in advance with the teacher.

Reviewing student writing

There is no spur for improvement quite like sharing your paragraph or hearing it read in the class. Whenever possible, completed student paragraphs should be presented to the class for evaluation and discussion. Of course, this can be done so that the writer is anonymous—and always with the concept that "there are no perfect paragraphs, and each paragraph contains strong and weak aspects" foremost in the students' minds. Lists of topic sentences, summary sentences, and grammatically troubled sentences also make stimulating in-class exercises.

Incorporating teacher's suggestions

The point of teacher correction is, of course, that students should improve their writing by incorporating their teacher's comments into their paragraphs. Each paragraph corrected by the teacher should be rewritten by the student. (Even advanced students can be encouraged to elevate their already excellent paragraphs with varied sentence length and structure.)

Ideally, during the class hour spent on incorporation, the teacher should try to find time to discuss briefly each student's main problems or to discuss the teacher's corrections on a one-to-one basis. Students should keep a file of their old paragraphs and be given some time each week to review past strengths and weaknesses.

To the Student

The purpose of writing is communication. When people write, they give their ideas and information to their reader or readers. In all major fields of study, research, and business, it is extremely important for a person to be able to communicate well in writing.

The purpose of this book is to show you how to communicate your ideas and information clearly in *paragraph* form. Learning to write paragraphs is an intermediate step in the process that ranges from writing sentences to writing essays. If you have studied writing before, you may already know something about paragraph form and the parts of the paragraph. In this book, you will study the parts of the paragraph intensively, and you will learn different types of writing, such as description and argument. These types of writing are merely devices for enabling you to communicate your ideas more clearly and effectively.

This book is based on model paragraphs written by other ESL students. These models and numerous writing activities are designed to stimulate your ideas about writing. However, *you should always remember that your writing will improve more through the writing and revising of your own paragraphs than through what you do in this book.*

Two important points:

1. The reader or readers of your writing are called your audience. The ideas, vocabulary, and sentence structure you use in writing depends on your audience. For example, if you were writing a paragraph about "The Economic Problems of My Country," the ideas and information you would include would depend on whether your audience consisted of people from your country. For the purposes of this book, always assume your reader is a person of intelligence and experience at least equal to your own (if not more than) in all subjects general and specific.

2. Try to make good use of Appendix B, the checklist for evaluating your own work. Remember that when you write, the quality of your ideas and information and your ability to communicate are most important. Moreover, your ideas and information cannot be communicated well if there are numerous problems with form and grammar. Writing is not about form and grammar, but form and grammar are of crucial importance in good writing.

Finally, the process of becoming a good writer is neither easy nor quick. It requires hard work and perseverance. Improvement often takes place gradually—so gradually that the writer cannot recognize it. And yet the reward is well worth the wait; the ability to communicate your ideas clearly and effectively will bring you a great sense of satisfaction.

Good writing!

Acknowledgments

I would like to thank the many students in my composition classes in the English for Foreign Students Program at the University of California–Davis who made contributions to this book and who endured the earlier, rougher versions of *Paragraph Power*.

In particular, I would like to thank and acknowledge the following students who contributed to the sample paragraphs used in this book: Urs Rudiger, Alphonso Novillo, Ernesto Lopez, Graciella Chang, Abu Moussa, Rodrigo Britto, Yoko Kamikawa, Holger Jessen, Monika Gerber, Michiko Kuki, Yumiko Aoyagi, Kunie Uenishi, Erik Algvere, and Mike Tanabe. Among these students are some of the best writers it has been my pleasure to teach.

Every paragraph in this book is the product of a collaborative effort by student writers. Again, to all my students, thank you for making this book possible.

Finally, I would sincerely like to thank my editor, Noël Vreeland Carter, for her many invaluable suggestions in putting together this second edition. Her highly professional creativity and diligence were key elements in bringing this project to fruition.

Paragraph Power

Chapter 1

What Is a Paragraph?

This chapter explains what a paragraph is and how an English paragraph may differ from writing in other languages.

The Nature of the English Paragraph

LET'S TALK ABOUT IT! *Introduce yourself to one or more of your classmates. When your classmate answers one of your questions, try to make conversation before moving on to the next question. For example, after receiving an answer to the first question, you might follow up with other questions such as* How old are you?, What do you do in your country? *or* How many brothers and sisters do you have? *before moving on to the second question.*

1. What's your name, and what country do you come from?
2. Where do you live in your country?
3. Tell me two things you like about the place where you live.
4. Tell me two things you don't like about the place where you live.
5. If I were going to visit your hometown, what would you show me? Tell me about three places you would take me and why.

    a. What is the best place to visit in your country?

    b. What are two reasons why this place is so nice?

6. What has been the best vacation that you have ever had? What were three things that you did on your vacation?
7. I am going to give you $10,000,000. You have one year to visit one place in the world that you have never been to. Where will you go? Why?
8. Look at the picture of Hawaii. What are three things that the people are doing? Would you like to go to the place in the picture? Why or why not?

1.1 Example

ACTIVITY 1 *Read the following paragraph and analyze it by completing the table on page 4. Then answer the following questions:* Which sentence gives the general subject and specific parts? How many sentences explain Parts 1 and 2? What kind of sentence comes after Part 2?

WHY DO SO MANY PEOPLE VISIT HAWAII?

Over a million people visit Hawaii each year because of the beautiful weather and wonderful scenery. The Hawaiian islands have very mild temperatures. For example, August, the hottest month, averages 78.4°F, while February, the coldest month, averages 71.9°F. In addition, the rainfall in Hawaii is not heavy because mountains on the northern side of each island stop incoming storms; for instance, Honolulu averages only 23 inches of rain per year. This beautiful weather helps tourists to enjoy Hawaii's incredible natural scenery, from mountain waterfalls to fields of flowers and pineapples. One unusual place on Kauai is the Waimea Canyon, which looks like the Grand Canyon in Arizona. Moreover, one of the world's largest volcanoes, Haleakala, is located on Maui. And, of course, Hawaii's famous beaches are everywhere—from the lovely Kona coast beaches on the large island of Hawaii to Waikiki Beach on Oahu. Warm sunshine and beautiful beaches—it is not surprising that so many people visit Hawaii each year.

Analysis

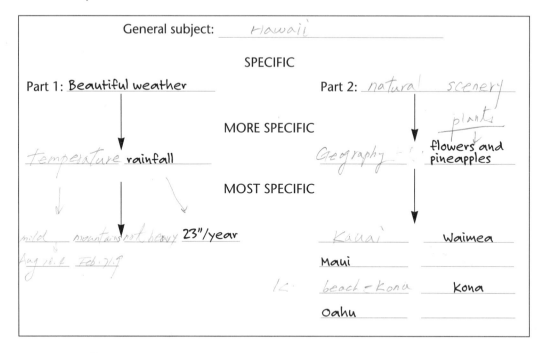

General subject: _Hawaii_

SPECIFIC

Part 1: Beautiful weather   Part 2: _natural scenery_

MORE SPECIFIC

plants

temperature rainfall   _Geography_   flowers and pineapples

MOST SPECIFIC

mild _mountains not heavy_ 23"/year   _Kauai_   Waimea

Aug 18.4 Feb. 71.9

Maui

beach - Kona   Kona

Oahu

1.2 *The two main types of writing*

Two of the main types of writing are personal writing and nonpersonal writing. In personal writing, *the writer ("I") is emphasized.* Personal writing is used in personal letters, on application forms, in literature, and in university writing courses.

In nonpersonal writing, *the subject of the writing is emphasized.* The paragraph about Hawaii is an example of nonpersonal writing because the subject (Hawaii) is emphasized. Nonpersonal writing is used in academic subjects such as physics, history, mathematics, engineering, economics, agriculture, business, and medicine.

In this book there are examples of both personal and nonpersonal writing. *The main focus of the book,* however, *is nonpersonal writing.* The primary purposes of nonpersonal writing are to explain and to persuade.

1.3 *The most important unit of English composition*

The most important unit of explanatory and persuasive writing in English is the *paragraph.* Compositions, reports, abstracts, summaries, and research papers are made up of many paragraphs.

1.4 The definition of a paragraph

A paragraph is a group of sentences which develop one subject logically .

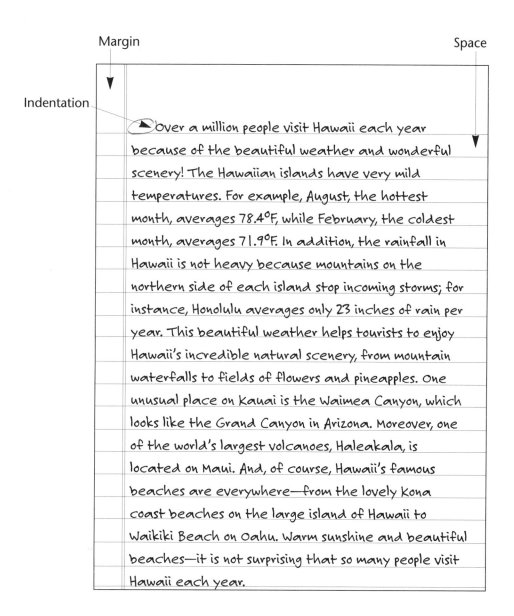

Figure 1.1 One paragraph on a regular 8 1/2 x 11 inch notebook page

The Form of the English Paragraph

1.5 The length and appearance of a paragraph

A paragraph is *a group of sentences*. The number of sentences in the paragraph depends on its subject. A paragraph with a simple subject may have <u>five sentences,</u> but a paragraph about a difficult subject may have ten sentences.

In this book you should write average-length paragraphs. Research has shown that the average paragraph in English has <u>five to ten sentences, with 75 to 150 words.</u> How many sentences were in the paragraph about Hawaii? *9*

Figure 1.1 on page 5 shows the main way these five to ten sentences may look on a regular notebook page. Notice the indentation at the beginning of the paragraph. It is important to realize that *many writers in the sciences and business do not use indentation;* instead, they begin the first line of the paragraph on the margin and skip a line between paragraphs. Whether you use the indentation is matter of personal choice, but either use it or don't use it every time you write a paragraph. Discuss your choice with your teacher.

Also, see that there are no breaks in the paragraph. A paragraph *runs <u>continuously</u>* from the first sentence to the last sentence. For neatness, leave a small space at the right of each line as you reach the edge of the page.

ACTIVITY 2   Now analyze Figure 1.2 on the next page. What is the problem with Paragraph 1 in the figure? What is the problem with the form of Paragraph 2?

Remember: *It is not necessary to indent paragraphs in scientific and business writing.*

Problem with Paragraph 1 _____

_____

Problem with Paragraph 2 _____

_____

Over a million people visit Hawaii each year because of the beautiful weather and wonderful scenery! The Hawaiian islands have very mild temperatures. For example, August, the hottest month, averages 78.4°F, while February, the coldest month, averages 71.9°F.

Poor Paragraph 1

In addition, the rainfall in Hawaii is not heavy because mountains on the northern side of each island stop incoming storms; for instance, Honolulu averages only 23 inches of rain per year.

This beautiful weather helps tourists to enjoy Hawaii's incredible natural scenery, from mountain waterfalls to fields of flowers and pineapples.

Poor Paragraph 2

One unusual place on Kauai is the Waimea Canyon, which looks like the Grand Canyon in Arizona.

Moreover, one of the world's largest volcanoes, Haleakala, is located on Maui.

Figure 1.2 Paragraphs with problems

Logical Paragraph Development in English

1.6 *Logical paragraph development in other languages*

A paragraph is a group of sentences *that develops logically* one subject. However, each language has a different logical pattern. In other words, Arabic has a different logical pattern from that of Spanish. English has a different logical pattern from those of Arabic and and Spanish. For example, study the logical patterns shown in Figure 1.3.

It is not logical for a Chinese (Mandarin) writer to develop a subject directly. Instead, a Chinese writer begins on the outside of the subject, develops the subject indirectly, and ends with the exact subject. Thus, *in Mandarin Chinese, logical development is indirect development.*

In contrast, it is logical for a writer of English to develop a subject directly. A writer of English usually begins with the exact subject, develops the subject directly with examples and facts, and ends with a summarizing sentence. Therefore, *in English, logical development is direct development.*

ENGLISH	SEMITIC	ORIENTAL	ROMANCE	RUSSIAN

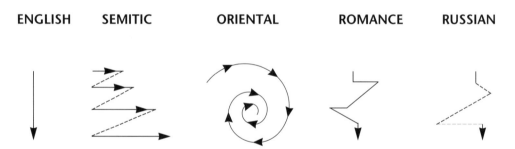

Figure 1.3 Logical development patterns of different cultures (From Robert B. Kaplan, *"Cultural Thought Patterns in Intercultural Education,"* Language Learning, 16: 15.) Reprinted by permission.

ACTIVITY 3   The following paragraph is written with the Asian *method of development. Read the paragraph carefully; then answer the questions.*

MY FAVORITE HISTORICAL PERIOD

As a child, some of my favorite novels were exciting science fiction ones such as *Dune* by Frank Herbert and *Journey to the Center of the Earth* and the *Time Machine* by Jules Verne. By reading these books I could imagine being transported to strange places in time. *Dune* was about a strange alien world of the future while the Verne novels were usually about going to strange places in the past. In *Journey to the Center of the Earth* the characters travel back in time as they go further into the Earth. As they near the Earth's center, they discover an exotic prehistoric world that time has forgotten. About the time that I was reading these books, I also became interested in Godzilla. I remember that when I first saw the movie *Godzilla*, I was very impressed with the size of the creature and its unusual characteristics, such as the fact that it was a vegetarian. Reading science fiction novels and watching such movies soon had giant flying reptiles, huge lizards, and dinosaurs running or flying through my imagination. Maybe that is the reason I decided to become a zoologist. For all these reasons and others, if I could travel back in time to another historical period, I would go to the Prehistoric Age. It would be incredibly exciting to try to survive along side the dinosaurs and it would be fascinating as a zoologist to study such animals.

Analysis

1. Look back at the paragraph about Hawaii. The first sentence of that paragraph communicates specifically what will be developed in the remainder of the paragraph (beautiful weather, wonderful scenery). Does the first sentence of the Asian paragraph tell specifically what will be discussed in the remainder of the paragraph?

   Explain _____

   _____

2. What is the relationship between *Journey to the Center of the Earth* and *Godzilla*?

   _____

3. Where does the writer give the main point of the paragraph?

   _____

ACTIVITY 4   A paragraph on the same subject using the Latin or Romance *method of development appears below. As you can see from Figure 1.3, the Latin method is closer in form to the English method than to the Asian method. The main difference is that writers using the Latin method often include sentences that are not directly related to the point. Cross out four sentences in the paragraph that are not directly related to the subject.*

MY FAVORITE HISTORICAL PERIOD

If I had a time machine, I would choose to go to the Prehistoric World because of the excitement, the food, my ability to see the future, and the possibility of scientific discovery. Imagine standing with an ax, wearing a yellow bikini made from wild animal fur with black spots. Of course, I really don't wear bikinis that much, I would never wear clothes with animal fur. How exciting! Imagine going out every day to hunt mammoths or dinosaurs, and never knowing if you would live or die—what a thrill! More than this, can you imagine eating the meat that you had killed; how do you think a low-fat brontosaurus steak would taste? It would be great for my diet! But how could I cook it? Would there be soy sauce in the Prehistoric World? Of course I wouldn't have to cook it myself because I'd be the most important person in the clan. I could foretell the future. The other members of the clan would make a religious group named after me called Mika Tanabe-Kyo. They would think I was a genius. Actually I do have an IQ of 143. But, on the other hand, it is doubtful whether they would believe all of the things that I would tell them. Finally, I would love the Prehistoric World because I am a zoologist and could investigate many extinct animals such as mammoths, dodos, and Japanese wolves. I am going to work on my master's degree in zoology starting in Spring Quarter. I am sure I would be able to discover new species of animals that we don't even know about today. Yes, the Prehistoric World would be the world for me—except for no air-conditioning and no ice cream—maybe I would rather stay at home!

1.7 The two types of direct logical development in English

In English, two types of paragraph are logical and direct: *inductive paragraphs* and *deductive paragraphs*. Since deductive paragraphs are the most common paragraphs in English, they will be explained in this book.

A deductive paragraph has three parts that provide direct logical development. Proportionately, these parts appear in the paragraph as shown in Figure 1.4.

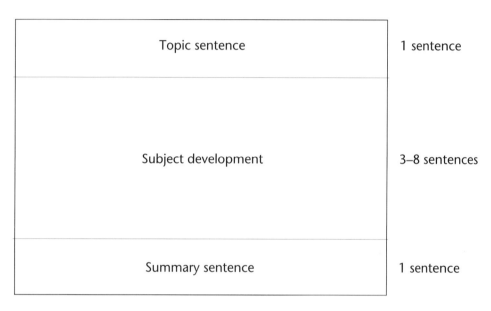

Figure 1.4 The three parts of a deductive paragraph.

ACTIVITY 5   The following paragraph, like the paragraph about Hawaii, uses the English style of direct development. As you read it, notice the topic sentence, subject development, and summary sentence. When you finish, complete the analysis.

MY FAVORITE HISTORICAL PERIOD

If I had a time machine, I would choose to go to the Prehistoric World because of the excitement, the food, my ability to see the future, and the possibility of scientific discovery. Imagine standing with an ax, wearing a yellow bikini made from wild animal fur with black spots. How exciting! Imagine going out everyday to hunt mammoths or dinosaurs, and never knowing if you would live or die—what a thrill! More than this, can you imagine eating the meat that you had killed; how do you think a low-fat brontosaurus steak would taste? It would be great for my diet! But how could I cook it? Would there be soy sauce in the Prehistoric World? Of course I wouldn't have to cook it myself because I'd be the most important person in the clan. I could foretell the future. The other members of the clan would make a religious group named after me called Mika Tanabe-Kyo. They would think I was a genius. But, on the other hand, it is doubtful whether they would believe all of the things that I would tell them. Finally, I would love the Prehistoric World because I am a zoologist and could investigate many extinct animals such as mammoths, dodos, and Japanese wolves. I am sure I would be able to discover new species of animals that we don't even know about today. Yes, the Prehistoric World would be the world for me—except for no air-conditioning and no ice cream—maybe I would rather stay at home!

Analysis

Point 1: _____	Specific
hunting	More|Specific
mammoths	▼ Most Specific

Point 2: _____	Specific
meat you have killed	More|Specific
_____	▼ Most Specific

Point 3: _____	Specific
new religious group	More|Specific
Mika Tanabe-kyo	▼ Most Specific

Point 4: _____	Specific
investigate extinct animals	More|Specific
_____ dodos _____	▼ Most Specific

ACTIVITY 6 *Discuss each one of the following situations with a group of your classmates. First, each person tells what he or she would do in the situations outlined below. Group members can ask follow-up questions before the next person speaks. Finally, the group should consider answers to the questions listed at the end of each situation.*

SITUATION 1: EATING OUT

You are eating in a very expensive restaurant. The service is terrible! Your waiter is incredibly slow and nasty. After you have finished eating, what will you do?

A. tell the waiter the service was awful
B. tip him the minimum 10% and say nothing
C. tell the manager about the waiter's poor service
D. tell and tip the waiter nothing

1. Describe poor service that you have experienced at a restaurant or elsewhere. What did you do?
2. If you were the manager of a restaurant and a customer complained about a waiter's poor service, what would you do?

SITUATION 2: A BIRTHDAY PARTY

A friend of yours is having a birthday party in your country. The invitation notes that the party will begin at 7:30. When will you arrive?

A. 7:00
B. 7:30
C. between 7:45 and 8:00
D. sometime after 8:00

1. Is time important in your country? What happens if a worker arrives fifteen minutes late for work? Thirty minutes? An hour?

2. If you were having a party and you wanted everyone to come by 9:00, what time of arrival would you put on the invitations?

SITUATION 3: IN CLASS

You are taking a required mathematics class at the university, and you are doing very badly. You just took the first exam, and you made an F. Your professor is extremely hard and not very friendly. What will you do?

A. Make an appointment with your professor to discuss your problem.
B. Try to get help from some of your classmates, and study harder.
C. Hire a private tutor.
D. Go to the math department and try to drop the class and retake it next quarter.

1. What was the worst class you ever had? What grade did you make?
2. How friendly do you think teachers should be with students? Very friendly, friendly, so-so friendly, not very friendly, or not friendly at all? Explain.

SITUATION 4A: A GUEST

You are forty years old, married with one child. Tonight you are a guest at your friend's house. Eating at the table are your friend and her husband (they are the same age as you and your spouse), your friend's grandmother (age 85), your friend's uncle (age 78), and of course you and your family. The food is on the table. Whom do you expect to be served first?

A. your friend and her husband (the hosts)

B. you, your spouse, and your child (the guests)

C. your friend's grandmother (the oldest) or uncle (the oldest man)

D. you will all begin to be served at the same time

SITUATION 4B: A GUEST

You are invited to your boss's house for dinner. What should you do?

A. bring some candy for the boss's children and some flowers for the boss's spouse

B. bring a bottle of wine

C. ask your boss if you can bring something

D. bring nothing

1. In your country, do people often eat at another person's home? Describe what happens if they do.

2. Has anyone ever acted impolitely in your home? If yes, what did they do? If no, what are three things that you would consider impolite?

3. Rank the following behaviors in order of impoliteness.

   1 = extremely impolite   8 = not very impolite

   _____ burping at the table
   _____ telling the host that the food doesn't taste good
   _____ eating food from a friend's plate
   _____ taking more food without the host's permission
   _____ talking with your mouth full
   _____ eating meat with your hands
   _____ wiping your mouth with your shirt
   _____ using your fingers to push food onto your fork

SITUATION 5: FINDING A SEAT

You are trying to find a seat in the university library. All of the tables and chairs are full except one table. It is occupied as shown in the diagram below. (M = Man and W = Woman)

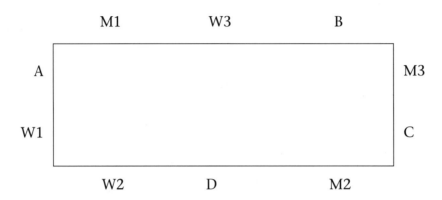

Where would you choose to sit?

A. in seat A
B. in seat B
C. in seat C
D. in seat D

1. Where did you choose to sit in the classroom today? Explain why you sat there. Do you sit in different places in different classrooms? Explain.
2. What are the classroom customs in your country? (Include customs relating to clothes, times, and speaking in class.)

Revision and Editing

1.8 Paragraph improvement

Good writers are constantly revising what they want to communicate and how they want to communicate it. In other words, revision takes place throughout the writing process—from the time the topic sentence is written until the summary sentence is completed. Ideas are formed, written down, and sometimes discarded. Sentences are written and rewritten until the writer is satisfied with their structure.

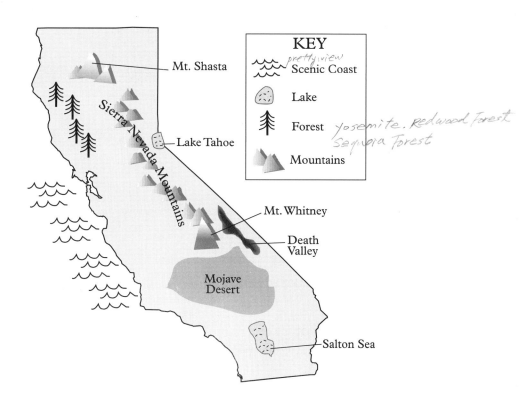

ACTIVITY 7   Imagine that you have been working on the following paragraph for the last hour, sharpening and refining your ideas and experimenting with various sentence structures. You now have a rough draft written, and you want to make a final revision that focuses the subject clearly and develops the idea completely. Read the paragraph and answer the questions that follow. Then revise the paragraph, adding the necessary information to communicate the idea fully to the reader.

THE BEST PLACE TO VISIT

California is the most wonderful place to visit because of its variety of weather and its beautiful nature. Visitors to California can find any weather they like. They can find cool temperatures in the summer; also they can find warm weather in the winter. They can find places that are difficult for humans to live in in the summer because they are so hot. Or they can find places closed in the winter because of the snow. On the other hand, visitors can find the nature they like. They can find high mountains and low valleys. Visitors can find a huge forest, a dead desert, and a beautiful coast. So California is the most wonderful place to visit because of its weather and nature.

1. Write a new title that focuses on the subject of the paragraph.

   Wondeful California

2. In your opinion, is this rough draft too general or too specific? *final draft => loot paper no mistakes.*

   Too general   *fist time you write a paper*

   Explain:

   no tetails, no specific places, no. names.

3. How can you make the third sentence more specific?

   Many of play ground at thou california

4. Using the map of California on page 17, give examples of the following natural features that are found in California:

   high mountains: _see page 17_

   deep valleys: _____

   a huge forest: _____

   a desert: _Mojave_

   a beautiful coast (between two cities): _Central California Coast_

5. Now revise the rough draft.

Wondeful California

California is the most wonderful place to visit
because of its variety of weather, beautiful nauture and play
ground.

1.9 Sentence correction

Most writers usually wait until a final revision has been made to edit their writing—check for problems with capitalization, punctuation, spelling, and grammar. Throughout this book, you will be asked to edit sentences for punctuation and grammatical mistakes.

ACTIVITY 8   *Each of the following sentences has one mistake. Find the mistake and correct it.*

1. For example, the Pyrenees <u>Mountains</u> and the Mediterranean <u>beaches</u> *are* in Spain.

Edited: _____

_____

2. Second, the stores in New York is very sophisticated. *S – v. agreemt.*

Edited: _____ *are* _____

_____

3. Disneyland has many things to do it has many rides, restaurants, and amusements.

   Edited: _____

   _____

4. Every summer many tourist visit Brazil because of its interesting people and its cheap prices.

   Edited: _____

   _____

5. Paris is lovely at the spring.

   Edited: _____

   _____

6. There are many beautiful islands such as a Canary Islands.

   Edited: _____

   _____

7. One of the most exciting city in the world is Seoul.

   Edited: _____

   _____

8. Nepal have high mountains and deep valleys.

   Edited: _____

   _____

9. In Kenya, wild animals and interesting scenery.

   Edited: _____

   _____

10. For this reason, people don't go there no more.

    Edited: _____

    _____

Application

1.10 *Writing assignment*

Write a paragraph in which you explain an idea by using examples. First, choose one of the following factual or imaginative topics for your paragraph.

Factual topics

city of your country.

1. Write a paragraph about a good or bad city or country to visit. In the topic sentence, be sure to give the name of the city or country and two reasons why that city or country is great or terrible for the visitor. *Choose a city or country that you have lived in so you can give many specific examples!* Use the paragraph about Hawaii as a model for your paragraph.

2. Write a paragraph about two or three important customs for a visitor to your country to know about. In the topic sentence, be sure to give the name of your country and a short, one- or two-word, description of each custom. You might write about some of the subjects you discussed in Activity 6.

Imaginative topic

Imagine that you could live at any time in the past. For example, imagine that you lived in China during the reign of Kublai Khan, Arabia at the time of Mohammed, Greece at the time of Plato and Socrates, Italy at the time of Michelangelo and daVinci, Peru during the rule of the Incas, or France under Louis XIV. Write a paragraph about the time you choose. In the topic sentence, provide two reasons for your choice. Include as many details about life then as possible. Use the paragraph in Activity 5 as an example.

Plan your paragraph carefully before you begin your writing. (You might talk over your ideas with a classmate or with the class as a whole.) Then write a rough draft—revising as you write. When you have finished, share your writing with one of your classmates. Have the classmate use Appendix B in the back of the book to evaluate your paragraph. What does your classmate think? Are there any points that he or she thinks are unclear? How can you better communicate your ideas?

Make any revisions that are desirable or necessary. Then edit your paragraph, using Appendix B as your guide. Submit your final copy to your teacher.

Chapter 2

The Parts of a Paragraph

This chapter presents the three parts of the paragraph and how these parts are developed and interconnected.

The Topic Sentence

LET'S TALK ABOUT IT!   *Ask one of your classmates each of the following questions. The person answering should give two or three reasons for his or her answer. The answers should be in topic sentence form. Try to make a conversation by following up each answer with a comment or question before moving on.*

> *Example:*
>
> Student A: Which car would you rather own, a Ferrari or a Honda?
>
> Student B: I would rather own a Honda because it's cheaper and gets better gas mileage.
>
> Student A: Come on, give me a break! Are you crazy? A Ferrari is a much better car because it's more stylish and faster.
>
> Student B: (Continues conversation)

1. Which musical group is your favorite?
2. Why are you studying English?
3. Would you rather be a dog, a fish, or a fly?
4. Would you rather live in India, Russia, or South Africa?
5. What is the best movie you've ever seen?
6. Which country will be the most powerful in the world in the year 3000?
7. Would you rather go to Hawaii, Switzerland, or Egypt on your next vacation?
8. Which period of history would you most like to have lived in?
9. Would you rather marry a beautiful or handsome person with a terrible personality or an extremely ugly person with a wonderful personality?
10. You are traveling through a small town, and you are very hungry. There are only three restaurants in the town: Chinese, Italian, and French. Where would you rather eat?
11. Which one of your grandparents do or did you like the most?
12. What is the most important holiday in your country?
13. If you were going to be alone on an island for the next 25 years, which ONE book would you carry with you?
14. Who is your favorite athlete?
15. Of all the subjects you have studied, which one was your *least* favorite?

2.1 The general subject and the specific parts

The first sentence of every paragraph you write in this book should be the topic sentence. The topic sentence communicates the subject of the paragraph by giving the reader *the general subject* and *the specific parts of the general subject* that will be developed in the paragraph.

For example:

1. The recent improvement in the American economy can be seen
   └─────────────── general subject ────────────────┘
   in the car, housing, and electronics industries.
   └──────────── specific parts ──────────┘

2. After a large star cools and collapses,
   └──────── specific parts ────────┘
   a black hole is formed in space.
   └──────── general subject ───────┘

3. Over a million people visit Hawaii each year
   └──────── general subject ────────┘
   because of its beautiful weather and wonderful scenery.
   └──────────── specific parts ──────────┘

Notice that either the general subject or the specific parts can appear first in the sentence. Read the two sentences that follow. Are they good topic sentences?

1. Foreign students come to the United States for two main reasons.

2. Kobe Bryant is the most exciting basketball player today.

What is the general subject of each sentence? What are the specific parts of each sentence? Do you know exactly what will be in the subject development of each? Explain.

_____

_____

_____

Both of these sentences give the reader the general subject. However, neither of them gives the reader the specific parts of the subject that will be developed.

In sentence 1, what are the two main reasons?

In sentence 2, why is Kobe Bryant the most exciting basketball player today?

Although these topic sentences are incomplete, we can change them into complete topic sentences by adding the specific parts:

1. Foreign students some to the United States primarily
   └────────────── general subject ──────────────┘
   to experience American culture and to attend an American university.
   └────────────────── specific parts──────────────────┘

2. Kobe Bryant's ball handling, creativity, and shooting make him
   └────────────── specific parts ──────────────┘
   the most exciting basketball player player today.
   └────────────── general subject ──────────────┘

ACTIVITY 1 *Using the preceding sentences as examples, change the following general sentences into complete topic sentences by adding the specific parts. Put as much variety into the sentences as you can. Use the questions in the parentheses to guide you.*

> *Example:* Businesses can offer their employees many benefits.
> (What benefits?)
> Health insurance, vacation time, and yearly bonuses
> └────────────── specific parts ──────────────┘
> are benefits that businesses can offer their employees.
> └────────────── general subject ──────────────┘

1. The camera has several important parts. (*Which parts?*)

   The camera has several important parts such as
   general subject

   _____

   specific parts

2. Soccer is the most popular sport in the world. (*Why?*)

Soccer is the most popular sport in the world because

———————————————————————————————

 general subject

———————————————————————————————
specific parts

3. The Internet can have negative effects on children. (*What effects?*)

———————————————————————————————
specific parts

are some of the negative effects the Internet has on children.
general subject

4. The 20th century has had some of the worst dictators in history.
(*Which ones?*)

———————————————————————————————
specific parts

were some of the worst dictators in history.
general subject

5. The developing countries are faced with many problems.
(*What problems?*)

———————————————————————————————
specific parts

———————————————————————————————
general subject

6. Scientists must develop new forms of energy. (*Which forms?*)

———————————————————————————————
general subject

———————————————————————————————
specific parts

The Subject Development

2.2 *Proper organization of the subject development*

The specific parts of the topic sentence organize the subject development. Consider one of the previous examples.

Kobe Bryant's ball handling, creativity, and shooting make him
└──────────────────── specific parts ────────────────────┘
the most exciting basketball player today.
└──────────── general subject ────────────┘

The subject development that comes from this topic sentence will have three parts, in specific order. What are the parts? What is the order?

Topic sentence	Kobe Bryant's ball handling, creativity, and shooting make him the most exciting basketball player today.
Subject development 3–8 sentences	1. ball handling 2. creativity 3. shooting
Summary sentence	

ACTIVITY 2   *Study the other topic sentence example and write a paragraph outline for it in the box below.*

Topic sentence	Foreign students come to the United States primarily to experience American culture and to attend an American university.
	1.
Subject development	2.
Summary sentence	

ACTIVITY 3   *Analyze the box below. What are the problems with the paragraph outline?*

Businesses can offer their employees many benefits such as health insurance, vacation time, yearly bonuses, and housing.
1. vacation time
2. housing
3. health insurance

Problems with outline: _____

_____

_____

2.3 Specific facts and specific examples

Deductive paragraphs move from the specific parts in the topic sentence to *more specific information* in the subject development.

Therefore, to complete the subject development, the most specific information about the subject is written down. The most specific kinds of information are *facts* (information and statistics) and *examples*.

ACTIVITY 4   *Provide examples, as directed, to support the italicized parts of the following topic sentences. Remember that after you have thought of, or found, a good example or fact, you must make that example or fact as specific as possible!*

A. When constructing roads in developing countries, engineers must use *a variety of road surfaces* and *machinery*.

    1. a variety of road surfaces

        Example 1: _____

        Example 2: _____

        Example 3: _____

    2. (a variety of) machinery

        Example 1: _____

        Example 2: concrete mixer _____

B. Students must take mathematics because of *its frequent use in everyday life* and *its fundamental importance to other sciences*.

    1. its frequent use in everyday life

        Example 1: at the gas station _____

        Example 2: _____

    2. its fundamental importance to other sciences

        Example 1: _____

        Example 2: _____

C. Studies have shown that most people today drink *too many non-nutritional drinks* and *eat too many junk foods.*

    1. too many non-nutritional drinks

        Example 1: _____

        Example 2: _____

    2. too many junk foods

        Example 1: *doughnuts* _____

        Example 2: _____

        Example 3: _____

D. Japanese car companies continue increasing their sales in the United States because of *their construction of smaller cars* and *their heavy use of many forms of advertising.*

    1. construction of smaller cars

        Example 1: _____

        Example 2: _____

        Example 3: _____

    2. many forms of advertising

        Example 1: *magazines* _____

        Example 2: _____

        Example 3: _____

E. Many movies of the 1990s and some planned for release in the first decade of the new century are *about science fiction* and *war.*

    1. movies about science fiction

        Example 1: _____

        Example 2: _____

        Example 3: _____

    2. movies about war

        Example 1: *"Saving Private Ryan"* _____

        Example 2: _____

        Example 3: _____

ACTIVITY 5 *Analyze the statistics in the following sentences. Which sentence is the least specific? Which sentence is the most specific?*

1. During the 1998 baseball season, Sammy Sosa and Mark McGwire both broke Roger Maris' homerun record.
2. In 1998, Sammy Sosa and Mark McGwire both broke Roger Maris' 37-year homerun record.
3. During the 1998 baseball season, with 66 and 70 homeruns respectively, Sammy Sosa and Mark McGwire both broke Roger Maris' 37-year record of 61 homeruns in one season.
4. In 1998, Sammy Sosa and Mark McGwire both broke Roger Maris' 37-year record of 61 homeruns in one season.

Least specific: _____

Why? _____

Most specific: _____

Why? _____

ACTIVITY 6 *Analyze the following pairs of sentences. Which pair contains the least specific example? Which pair contains the most specific example?*

Pair 1: Records show that within every age group, from infant to ninety years old, more females live than males. For example, in the United States, more girl babies survive the first year of life than boy babies.

Pair 2: Records show that within every age group, from infant to ninety years old, more females live than males. For example, United Nations statistics show that in the United States, three girl babies survive the first year of life for every 2.8 boy babies.

Pair 3: Records show that within every age group, from infant to ninety years old, more females live than males. For example, in countries throughout the world, more girl babies survive the first year of life than boy babies.

Pair 4: Records show that within every age group, from infant to ninety years old, more females live than males. For example, in the United States, three girl babies survive the first year of life for every 2.8 boy babies.

Pair 5: Records show that within every age group, from infant to ninety years old, more females live than males. For example, United Nations statistics show that in the period 1997-98 in the United States, three girl babies survived the first year of life for every 2.8 boy babies.

Least specific: _____

Why? _____

Most specific: _____

Why? _____

ACTIVITY 7 *Of the following groups of sentences (topic sentences and subject developments), which one is the better because it is the more specific?*

GROUP A

(*Topic sentence*) The battles of Marathon and Tours are examples of how war has often determined the development of Western civilization. (*Subject development*) The basis of Western civilization was probably decided in Greece at the Battle of Marathon in 490 B.C. In this battle, 10,000 Greek soldiers led by Miltiades defeated 100,000 invading Persians under Darius I. Because the Greeks won, Greek ideas about philosophy, science, literature, and politics (such as democracy) matured and became the foundation of Western society. Whereas Marathon laid the basis of Western civilization, its structure remained the same as a result of the Battle of Tours in A.D. 732. Before this battle, Muslim armies had taken control of countries from India to the Atlantic Ocean, but they were stopped by a European army under Charles Martel at this battle in southwestern France. If the Muslims had won at Tours, Islam might have become the major religion of Western society.

GROUP B

(*Topic sentence*) The battles of Marathon and Tours are examples of how war has often determined the development of Western civilization. (*Subject development*) The basis of Western civilization was probably decided in Greece at the Battle of Marathon about 2,500 years ago. In this battle, a small number of Greek soldiers led by a famous Greek general defeated 100,000 invading Persians under the Persian king. Because the Greeks won, Greek ideas about many subjects matured and became the foundation of Western society. Whereas Marathon laid the basis of Western civilization, its structure remained the same as a result of the Battle of Tours in A.D. 732. Before this battle, Muslim armies had taken control of a large number of countries, but they were stopped by a group of soldiers led by Charles Martel in France. If the Muslims had won at Tours, Islam might have become the major religion of Western society.

Analysis of Groups A and B

General fact in group: _____ ➝	Specific fact in group: _____
1. decided at the battle of	decided in Greece at the
2. about 2500 years ago	in 490 B.C.
3.	
4.	
5.	
6.	
7.	
8.	
9.	

Remember: Use the most specific information possible in the subject development.

The Summary Sentence

2.4 Methods of summarizing

In general, most summary sentences are constructed according to one of the two following methods:

Method 1: Repeat the main ideas of the paragraph in a new way.
Method 2: Give a conclusion based on the information in the paragraph.

Always write a strong summary sentence because it is the last sentence the reader sees. Summarizing with a question will provoke your reader to further thinking; an exclamatory sentence may add emphasis to your idea.

ACTIVITY 8   Look back at the two summary sentences used in the English method paragraphs in Chapter 1. Analyze them with respect to Method 1.

1. Write down the summary sentence of the paragraph about Hawaii on page 3.

    _____

    _____

    Which two main ideas are repeated in this sentence?

    _____

    <u>wonderful scenery</u>_____

2. Write down the summary sentence of the paragraph about a favorite historical period on page 12.

    _____

    _____

    What conclusions are given in this sentence?

    _____

    _____

ACTIVITY 9   *Review Group A on page 33. Write summary sentences below for Group A, using Methods 1 and 2.*

Summary sentence using Method 1:

_____

_____

_____

_____

_____

_____

Summary sentence using Method 2:

_____

_____

_____

_____

_____

_____

Language Patterns in the Paragraph

2.5 Creating continuous connections between sentences

A paragraph is a group of sentences that logically develop *one subject*. Because each sentence in the paragraph is about the same general subject, each sentence must be connected tightly to the sentence before it and to the sentences after it. To make the connections tight in your paragraphs, use *continuing* connectors and *transition* connectors. Every paragraph should have continuing and transition connectors.

2.6 Continuing connectors

A continuing connector is a word or phrase that shows that the specific subject of the sentence is still being discussed in the next sentence. There are three kinds of continuing connectors.

1. Repeated words and phrases

   Example: The gravitational force is so strong that no light or matter can come out from the point of collapse. Finally, because *no light* can be seen *at the point of collapse*, this area of space is called a black hole.

2. Demonstrative adjectives (*this, that, these, those*)

   Example: The first people probably came to North America from northern Asia about 12,000 years ago. *These* people crossed over a land bridge from northern Asia and traveled down through northwestern Canada into America.

3. Pronouns

   Example: These people crossed over a land bridge from northern Asia and traveled down through northwestern Canada into America. *They* remained by *themselves* for thousands of years.

ACTIVITY 10   Analyze this paragraph by underlining the continuing connectors that are used to make the sentences continuous and tight. The first three sentences have already been done.

HOW IS A BLACK HOLE FORMED?

1   After a large star cools and collapses, a black hole is formed.
2   First, as the nuclear fuel of a <u>star</u> runs out, <u>its</u> center begins to <u>cool</u>.
3   While <u>this</u> <u>cooling</u> is taking place, the <u>star</u> <u>begins</u> to <u>collapse</u>
4   inwardly because of the enormous mass of the <u>star's</u> outer layers. In
5   fact, if the star has a mass so great that the collapse cannot be
6   stopped, its collapse continues forever. The gravitational force of this
7   kind of collapse is so strong that no light or matter can come out
8   from the point of collapse. Finally, because no light can be seen at
9   the point of collapse, this area of space is called a black hole.

2.7 *Transition connectors*

The second type of connector is a transition connector. A transition connector is a word that shows that the subject of a sentence will be expanded or changed in the next sentence. The main transition words and the relationship they show are below:

RELATIONSHIP	EXAMPLES
1. consequence (result)	therefore, thus, as a result
2. comparison (likeness)	similarly, in the same way
3. contrast (difference)	but, however, on the contrary, on the other hand, conversely
4. example (illustration)	for example, for instance
5. restatement (repetition)	in other words
6. addition	in addition, also, moreover, furthermore
7. concession (even though)	nevertheless, nonetheless
8. sequence (order)	first, second, third, (etc.), to begin with, next, after
9. summary (conclusion)	in conclusion, to summarize, in summary

ACTIVITY 11 *Working with at least three of your classmates, create a story from each of the following first lines. Each person in order adds one line to the story, building upon what the previous person says. A transition word must be used at the beginning of each line. Each story should have at least twelve lines. Write down each line as you create the story so that you can compare them later with the stories of your classmates.*

Rule: *You cannot repeat any transition word within a story.*

Example: It was a dark, rainy night.

Student 1: Therefore, Mary decided to stay home.

Student 2: First, she decided to cook some steak and fries.

Student 3: Next, she walked to the refrigerator.

Student 1: However, when she opened the freezer, she found a dead person inside.

(and so on)

FIRST LINES:

1. It was a dark, rainy night.
2. Peter and Madonna thought they loved each other very much.
3. When all her money was gone, Mrs. Smith decided to rob a bank.
4. The students decided that they hated their teacher.
5. Scientists have discovered that the sun will explode in three days and that the earth will be destroyed.
6. Mohammed won $23,000,000 in the lottery yesterday.

ACTIVITY 12 Write an appropriate transition word in each blank to show the relationship in parentheses.

1. Some birds cannot fly well. _____, the chicken has wings, but its flying muscles are not strong enough to be useful. (*example*)

2. Einstein's general theory of relativity helped form the basis of modern physics. _____, the discoveries of physicists today would be much more difficult to make without Bohr's development of quantum mechanics. (*comparison*)

3. Plants that grow in high desert areas must live in extreme daytime heat. _____, they must be able to tolerate severe nighttime cold. (*addition*)

4. Korean factories produce electronic products inexpensively and efficiently. _____, Korea is one of the world's leading exporters of microwave ovens. (*consequence*)

5. Today the Himalayas are the highest mountains in the world. _____, geologists have shown that millions of years ago the Appalachian Mountains of the eastern United States were higher. (*contrast*)

6. The Humber Suspension Bridge in Hull, England, is the longest such bridge in the world. _____, the Golden Gate Bridge in San Francisco is the world's most famous suspension bridge. (*concession*)

ACTIVITY 13   *Write pairs of sentences to show the use of the transition relationships below.* The transition connector must be the first word of the second sentence. *Use the sentences in Activity 11 as examples.*

1. consequence _____

_____

_____

_____

2. consequence _____

_____

_____

_____

3. contrast _____

_____

_____

_____

4. contrast _____

_____

_____

5. comparison _____

_____

_____

6. concession _____

_____

_____

_____

7. addition _____

_____

_____

8. example _____

_____

_____

Revision and Editing

2.8 Paragraph improvement

ACTIVITY 14 Carefully read the following rough draft and answer the questions. Then revise the rough draft to improve the way in which the ideas are communicated.

WHAT ARE THE TWO HARDEST SECTIONS ON THE COMPUTER-BASED TOEFL TEST?

The Test of English as a Foreign Language (TOEFL) has three sections. The most difficult sections for me are listening comprehension and structure.

The structure section which now contains the TWE, is computer-adaptive. The section contains a mixture of two types of problems. In one type of problem, there is an incomplete sentence, and the testee must click on the word or phrase that best completes the sentence.

We arrived _____ late that there were no seats left.

   much   too   so   very

In the listening comprehension section, the testee chooses answers based on static photographs and audio of short conversations, long conversations, and mini-lectures. The listening comprehension section tests the students' ability to understand spoken English.

What is the problem with:

1. the paragraph form?

2. the topic sentence?

3. the information about the grammar section?

4. the information about the listening comprehension section?

_____

_____

5. the summary sentence?

_____

_____

6. the transition connectors?

_____

_____

Now revise the rough draft.

_____

_____

_____

_____

_____

_____

_____

_____

_____

_____

_____

_____

_____

_____

_____

_____

_____

2.9 Sentence correction

ACTIVITY 15 *Each sentence has one mistake. Find the mistake and correct it.*

1. Beethoven's piano sonatas and symphonies establishes his reputation as a great musician.

    Edited:

    _____

    _____

    _____

2. Martina Hingis's powerful backhand and return of serve make her the top tennis player in the late 1990s.

    Edited:

    _____

    _____

    _____

3. Russia was made into strong country by Peter the Great.

    Edited:

    _____

    _____

    _____

4. For example, Zico, Beckenbauer, and Pelé.

    Edited:

    _____

    _____

    _____

5. King Abdul-Aziz united the tribes of Arabia and he formed Saudi Arabia.

    Edited:

    _____

    _____

    _____

6. The entrance exam for the University of Beijing consisted of a difficult verbal section and a lot of easy questions about mathematics.

   Edited:

   _____

   _____

   _____

7. Michael Jordan is one of the best basketball player in history.

   Edited:

   _____

   _____

   _____

8. Because he developed the general theory of relativity.

   Edited:

   _____

   _____

   _____

9. Every year at Sweden there is a skiing contest in memory of Gustav Wasa.

   Edited:

   _____

   _____

   _____

10. Benito Juárez changed the course of Mexico because he made the reform laws he was born in Welato, Oaxaca in 1820.

    Edited:

    _____

    _____

    _____

Application

2.10 Writing assignment

Write a paragraph in which you explain an idea by using examples or statistics. Choose one of the following factual or imaginative topics for your paragraph.

Factual topics

1. Write a paragraph about a great scientist or artist (painter, musician, dancer, writer). In the topic sentence, give two or three qualities that make the person memorable. Include many examples (specific songs, paintings, books) in the subject development to illustrate your ideas.

2. Write a paragraph about one of the best players in a particular sport (baseball, soccer, tennis, for example). The player may be living or dead, active or retired. In the topic sentence give two or three characteristics that make (made) the player outstanding in his sport. Include as many specific statistics (batting average, fielding percentage, goals scored, speed of serve) as you can.

3. Write a paragraph about "How a Great Leader Can Determine the Course of a Country." Choose one person who established or change the course of your county's history. Then give at least two or three things that the person did. Use the sentences in Group A on page 35 as models.

Imaginative topic

Imagine that you are a great scientist, artist, sportsperson, or politician. How would your life be different? Give examples and details of how you would use your situation to better the world.

Plan your paragraph carefully in a small group setting before you begin your writing. Write down your main idea and as many examples as you can think of. When you have finished (in about 5–10 minutes), ask the people in your group what they think. Ask them if they think it is an interesting subject and if they have any examples or suggestions. Then write a rough draft, revising as you write. When you have finished, share your writing with one or more classmates. What do they think? Are there any points that they think are unclear? How can you better communicate your ideas?

Make any revisions that are desirable or necessary. Then edit your paragraph, using Appendix B. Submit your final copy to your teacher.

Chapter

3

Explanation by Description of an Object

This chapter explains the different aspects of describing an object, focusing on limiting the subject and describing the parts of the object.

The Nature of Description

Preliminary Considerations

Writing the Descriptive Paragraph

Special Grammar in Description

Revision and Editing

Application

The Nature of Description

LET'S TALK ABOUT IT!   GAME TIME! 21 Questions. Divide the class into teams. The teacher will assign categories such as animal, plant, furniture, classroom equipment, etc., to each team. The teams then huddle secretly for five minutes in order to choose three or more objects from their assigned category. The game then proceeds as follows:

Team 1 stands or sits in front of the class. The members of the other teams ask questions, in turn, trying to elicit information about the object or guessing what the object is. Questions can be either yes/no or informational. The teacher will keep track of how many questions have been asked. If the questioners cannot guess in twenty-one questions, then Team 1 scores a point. Then Team 2 continues the game.

3.1 Example

ACTIVITY 1   Read this example paragraph carefully. Then underline the transition words in the paragraph, label the various parts in the diagram, and complete the analysis.

A PIECE OF M&M'S® PEANUT CANDY

An M&M's® peanut candy is composed of a thin exterior layer of hardened sugar, a soft inner layer of chocolate, and a peanut in the middle. Overall, the piece of candy is oval-shaped, about 3/4" long, and 1/2" high, with a weight of approximately 5 grams. Moving from the outside to the inside, the piece of candy is covered by an extremely thin shell of hardened sugar. On the outside, the shell can be any one of several colors such as brown, blue, or red. The shell has three purposes: to make the piece of candy easy to hold, to contain the candy inside, and to advertise—the letters M&M® are printed on the outside of each shell. The shell itself is 1/32" thick and covers the entire piece of candy. Inside the shell is a soft layer of brown, chocolate candy which is about 3/32" thick. The chocolate is mainly composed of sugar, chocolate milk, cocoa butter, lactose, soy lecithin, and salt. Obviously the purpose of the chocolate is to provide the main "sweet" part of the candy. Inside the soft layer of chocolate, in the center of the piece of candy, is the peanut. The peanut is oval-shaped with a length of about 1/2" and a width of 1/4". Its weight is about 2 1/2 grams. The peanut provides a solid core for the candy and adds an element of crunchiness to its texture. Nutritionally speaking, 1/4 of a cup of pieces of M&M's® candy will provide the consumer with 17 percent of the recommended daily intake of fat, 9 percent of the recommended daily intake of carbohydrates, 4 percent of the recommended daily intake of dietary fiber, and 1 percent of the recommended daily intake of sodium. In summary, with its exterior layer of sugar, inner layer of chocolate, and peanut center, a piece of M&M's® candy is an elegantly designed, classic candy snack.

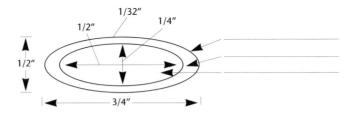

Diagram of an M&M's® peanut candy

Analysis

	Object: _____	
PART 1: ↓	PART 2: ↓	PART 3: ↓
	CHARACTERISTICS	
	USE/FUNCTION	

3.2 Explanation

A description of an object is an analysis of its parts. Each important part of the object is examined in a descriptive paragraph.

A description does not contain the feelings of the writer. Instead, the description of each part is factual. For example:

> *General:* The shell is very thin.
> *Specific:* The shell is 1/32" thick.

In a description, the physical characteristics of each part (size, weight, shape, etc.) are emphasized, and the function (use of each part) is mentioned. Descriptive paragraphs should follow the pattern below.

Title
Topic sentence
Part 1: Physical characteristics (and use) Part 2: Physical characteristics (and use) Part 3: Physical characteristics (and use) (Part 4: Same as above, if necessary)
Summary sentence
Diagram of object (with important parts and dimensions labeled)

Preliminary Considerations

3.3 Choosing a limited subject

The subject of a descriptive paragraph must be a limited object with a small number of important parts—usually something that can be held in the hand. For example, it is impossible to describe an airplane engine in one paragraph because it has too many important parts. Be specific in the title; instead of writing about "a tennis racket," write about a specific brand or kind, a "Prince 102 Tennis Racket," for instance.

ACTIVITY 2   *Which two of the following subjects are the most limited?*

1. A water oak tree

2. A Sears 1500-cubic-foot air conditioner

3. A Hyundai Lancia automobile engine

4. A GE 100-watt white light bulb

5. A preformatted 3.5 PC Disk

6. The leg of a housefly

ACTIVITY 3   *Write specific limited titles for four descriptive paragraphs.*

_____

_____

_____

_____

3.4 Descriptive order

After you have chosen the object you will describe, decide on the important parts of the object to be analyzed. The parts of the object can be organized in four main ways:

Vertical order: top to bottom or bottom to top
Horizontal order: left to right or right to left
Depth order: inside to outside or outside to inside
Circular order: clockwise or counterclockwise

For example, the writer of the M&M Candy paragraph used depth order as the organizational base of his description.

ACTIVITY 4   *Which order, or combination of orders, would you use to describe the parts of these objects?*

the bird nest of a California blue jay   _____

a Baden S350 soccer ball   _____

an Arabian teapot   _____

a Gerber baby bottle   _____

a Stradivarius violin   _____

a leaf from a Chinese cherry tree   _____

Remember, the main organizational point is to have an order in your mind when you describe the parts of your object. Do not describe the parts of the object randomly.

Writing the Descriptive Paragraph

3.5 The topic sentence

In the topic sentence of a descriptive paragraph, the general idea is the object, and the specific parts are the most important parts of the object. The specific parts are written down in the order they will be developed.

Examples: The tobacco, its wrapping paper, and the filter are
└─────────────── specific parts ───────────────┘
the most important parts of a Marlboro "light" cigarette.
└─────────────── general idea ───────────────┘

The center of a rose is composed of
└─────────── general idea ───────────┘
the stigma, the style, and the ovary.
└─────────── specific parts ───────────┘

ACTIVITY 5   *Write two topic sentences for a descriptive paragraph.*

1. _____

   are the three main parts of a pair of scissors.

2. _____

   _____

3.6 Language patterns in the topic sentence and subject development

The subject development of a descriptive paragraph details each part, shows how that part is related to the other parts, and explains the use of the part. Therefore, the patterns of composition, of spatial relationship, and function found on the next page are often used.

A. Language pattern to show the object and its parts

OBJECT		PARTS
An apple	is made of is made up of is composed of is comprised of contains consists of	a core of seed, the fruit, the skin, and the stem.

B. Language patterns to show the relationship of one part to another

ONE PART		ANOTHER PART
The stem	is attached to is connected to	the fruit of the apple.
The core of seeds	is surrounded by is enclosed in (by)	the fruit of the apple.
	(or)	
The fruit of the apple	surrounds encloses	the core of seeds.
The seeds	rest in are held in	a protective case.
	(or)	
A protective case	holds	the seeds.
The fruit of the apple	is covered by is protected by	a thin outer skin.
	(or)	
A thin outer skin	covers protects	the fruit of the apple.

Other words that show spatial relationship are:

outside/inside above/below next to/beside	extends from/under between	in front of/behind apart

C. Language pattern to show the function of the part

PART		FUNCTION
The seeds	are used to serve to	begin new plants.
The seeds	are responsible for perform the function of are used for	beginning new plants.

ACTIVITY 6   *Use the language patterns and sequence transition words to complete these sentences. Then complete the figure and analysis on page 58.*

WHAT ARE THE ELEMENTS OF A SOCCER GOAL?

A regulation soccer goal _____ three main parts: two goal posts, a crossbar, and a net. _____ , there are two goalposts (6–12 inches in circumference), which _____ hard plastic, fiber glass, or wood. They should be 8 yards _____ in the ground. These goalposts _____ establish the outer limits of the shot, _____ the crossbar, and _____ the net. _____ , the crossbar _____ the same material as the goalposts, and is 8 feet long and 8–12 inches in circumference. It _____ to the top of the goalposts by a suitable method (screws for plastic or nails for wood). The crossbar _____ as the uppermost limit of the shot and as a support for the net. _____ , the nylon net is rectangular; typical net dimensions are 16 x 18 feet. The net is _____ to the goal posts by strings of wire, and is staked into the ground _____ the goal line to stop balls after scores are made. A regulation goal is essential to the proper playing of a soccer game because it determines how points are scored.

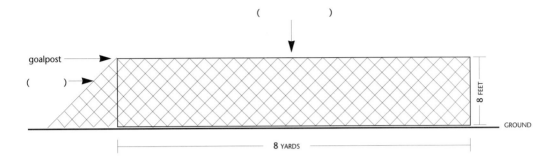

goalpost →

(   ) →

8 FEET

(   )

GROUND

8 YARDS

Regulation Soccer Goal (not to scale)

Analysis

Whole Object: _____

PART 1:   PART 2:   PART 3:

▼   ▼   ▼

CHARACTERISTICS

USE/FUNCTION

3.7 The summary sentence

The summary sentence of a descriptive paragraph should emphasize why the object is important.

Example: A regulation goal is essential to the proper playing of a soccer game because it determines how points are scored.

ACTIVITY 7 *Look back at the opening paragraph about the piece of M&Ms candy on page 50. The paragraph could have a stronger summary sentence. Rewrite the sentence below emphasizing why a piece of M&M candy might be important.*

_____

_____

_____

_____

3.8 The diagram

ACTIVITY 8 *Study Figure 3.1 carefully. Then, using the ruled lines on page 60, write a paragraph describing an American Supersteel No. 22 tack.*

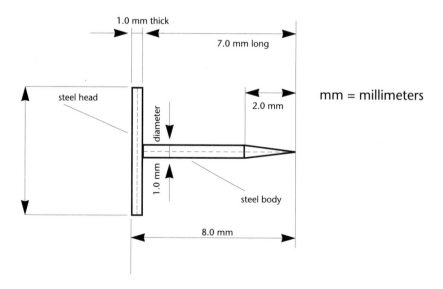

Figure 3.1 American Supersteel No. 22 tack

AN AMERICAN SUPERSTEEL NO. 22 TACK

_____

_____

_____

_____

_____

_____

_____

_____

_____

_____

_____

_____

_____

_____

_____

_____

_____

_____

_____

_____

_____

_____

ACTIVITY 9   *Below is a list of five objects. You and your team will have a total of 25 minutes to draw a detailed diagram of each object. Draw each one on a separate piece of paper. At the end of the time allotted, the class will judge each set of drawings. The winning drawings should be the ones that are the most detailed. The winning teams will receive a prize to be determined by the teacher.*

A no. 2 wooden pencil

A pair of glasses

An audio cassette (just the case)

A sock

A quarter (25 cents)

Special Grammar in Description

3.9 Use of the passive

As you saw in Section 3.6, writers often use the passive voice in descriptive paragraphs. The purpose of the passive voice is to communicate the importance of the object. There are many forms of the passive voice, but the most common form in description is:

Simple present passive: Object + is/are + past participle (+ *by* subject)

Example: Active   X-52 resin covers the bottom of the board.
└─subject─┘ └─verb─┘ └──────── object ────────┘

Passive   The bottom of the board   is covered
└──────── object ────────┘ + *is* + past participle

by X-52 resin.
└─ + *by* subject ─┘

Common passives in description include:

ACTIVE	PASSIVE	ACTIVE	PASSIVE
surrounds	is surrounded by	joins	is joined by
holds	is held by	supports	is supported by
covers	is covered by	protects	is protected by
fasten	is fastened by		

Unusual passives in description include:

ACTIVE	PASSIVE		
makes	is made *of*	→	(in the topic sentence)
consists of	is *composed of*	→	do not change the order of subject and object
rests on	is *supported* by		

ACTIVITY 10   *Change these sentences to passive.*

1. A soft rubber coating surrounds the Ping-Pong paddle head.

   Passive:

   _____

   _____

2. A colored woolen material with .1 inch thickness and nap surface covers the ball.

   Passive:

   _____

   _____

3. Two brass strips connect the switch to the negative battery terminal.

   Passive:

   _____

   _____

4. A person uses the rugged, narrow (.6 centimeter) line to light the match.

   Passive:

   _____ to light the match ___

   do not include the *by* subject

   _____

5. The new PX35 Special flashlight consists essentially of a bulb, a battery, and a switch.

   Passive:

   _____

   _____

ACTIVITY 11   *Using the ruled lines on page 63, rewrite the following paragraph, changing the italicized parts to passive.*

A ROSSIGNOL F. P. COMPETITION SNOW SKI

A Rossignol F. P. competition snow ski *consists of* the board and the edges. First, the board, which allows the skier to slide over the snow, has a special internal structure (see the diagram) made of hard plastic and metal. *Hard polymers make up the deck and hard bottom of the board.* Moreover, *slippery X-52 resin covers the bottom of the board.* The length of the board varies between 5 and 7 feet; its width is 2.5 inches, and its height is 0.45 inches. Second, *five screws attach the two edges* to each side of the bottom of the board. These edges permit controlled sliding and *consist of* sharp, rectangular steel rods. The length of each edge varies between 5 and 7 feet, and the thickness of each is about 0.002 inches. To summarize, this ski has such strong structure and good design that it is possible to use it to ski fast and surely on all kinds of slopes and snow.

Open Front View of Ski
(No Dimensions, Structure Emphasized)

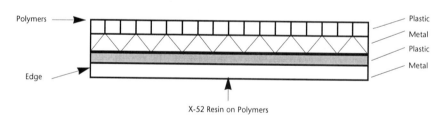

Internal structure of Rossignol F. P. Competition Snow Ski

A ROSSIGNOL F. P. COMPETITION SNOW SKI

_____

_____

_____

_____

_____

_____

_____

_____

_____

_____

_____

_____

_____

_____

_____

Revision and Editing

3.10 Paragraph improvement

ACTIVITY 12   Carefully read and then revise the following rough draft. Begin by answering the questions and use the answers to guide your revision.

A 12 OUNCE COCA-COLA® CAN

A 12 ounce aluminum Coca-Cola® can has a few important parts. To begin with, the empty can is pretty high with a circumference of over 8 inches. The can is recessed a little bit at the bottom and at the top. Normally the can is made of aluminum, and its purpose is to hold the Coke®. Next, there is a small, rectangular opener tab that is also made out of aluminum. Obviously, the tab performs the function of opening the can. Finally, there is a small metal pin between the can and the tab.

1. What is wrong with the topic sentence?

_____

2. What is the problem with the organizational order?

_____

3. What are four places at which a measurement should be given in order to make the paragraph more specific?

_____

_____

4. Is there any part whose function is not given?

_____

5. What is the problem with the summary sentence?

_____

_____

6. In the space below, draw a diagram of the object.

Now revise the rough draft.

3.11 Sentence correction

ACTIVITY 13 *Each sentence has one mistake. Find the mistake and correct it.*

1. Foster sunglasses are consists of a metal frame and two lenses.
   Edited:

   _____

   _____

   _____

2. From top to bottom, the plant has 2 centimeters long.
   Edited:

   _____

   _____

   _____

3. This imaginary animals have no ears and no eyes.
   Edited:

   _____

   _____

   _____

4. The cup which has a porcelain surface and weighs 400 grams.
   Edited:

   _____

   _____

   _____

5. At least ten seeds are usually inside the fruit of an orange.
   Edited:

   _____

   _____

   _____

6. The tips of the shoestring is made of thin plastic.

   Edited:

   _____

   _____

   _____

7. There are tiny hairs in the surface of the leg.

   Edited:

   _____

   _____

   _____

8. A gold necklace with a length of 10 centimeters and a width of
   100 millimeters.

   Edited:

   _____

   _____

   _____

9. The tops are covers by thick sheets of aluminum.

   Edited:

   _____

   _____

   _____

10. The side of the head is flat and the head is used to hit the nail.

    Edited:

    _____

    _____

    _____

Application

3.12 Team writing assignment

For this writing assignment, you will need to work with one of your classmates. First, choose an interesting object to describe. Use one of the suggestions below, or choose an object yourself with the approval of your teacher.

Factual topics

1. Write a paragraph describing a piece of sports or musical equipment, such as a baseball, tennis racket, Ping-Pong paddle, water ski, clarinet mouthpiece, violin bow, or piano key.

2. Write a paragraph describing a personal article you find in your home; for example a wallet, toothbrush, flashlight, cigarette lighter, necklace, pencil case, or stapler.

3. Write a paragraph describing a piece of scientific equipment, such as a drawing compass, a simple microscope, a pair of binoculars, a Bunsen burner, or a simple piece of laboratory equipment.

3. Write a paragraph describing a natural object such as a sea shell, flower, leaf, piece of bark, or plant stem.

Imaginative topic

Describe a small imaginary animal or plant scientifically. Include measurements to depict your creation in detail.

Draw a detailed diagram of the object with exact dimensions. Exchange diagrams with your classmate. Then write a rough draft based on your classmate's diagram—revising as you write.

After you have finished your rough draft, exchange drafts and diagrams with your classmate. What do you think? Did your classmate do a good job of writing a paragraph based on your diagram? Are there any points that are unclear? Discuss your ideas with your classmate. Revise your classmate's paragraph and edit it using Appendix B. Submit the final copy to your teacher.

Chapter 4

Directional Process Analysis

This chapter deals with writing a "how to" paragraph, including assessing relative importance and determining order.

The Nature of Process Analysis

LET'S TALK ABOUT IT! *Have a "how to" conversation with one of your classmates. Slowly and clearly, explain to each other how to do each of the following things. Each process should have at least seven steps. After your classmate describes the "how to" steps, try to repeat the process described. When the activity is over, your teacher may ask you to tell the class the "how to" process described by your classmate.*

Please tell me how to:

1. kiss a person of the opposite sex lovingly
2. kiss a person of the same or opposite sex as a greeting
3. ride a bicycle
4. tie a shoe
5. make an "A" in this class
6. be happy
7. make a lot of money
8. drive a car
9. play _____ (choose a sport)
10. meet Americans
11. spend a "free" day
12. take a bath

As a follow-up to this conversation, teach your classmates how to do something (*play a game, draw a picture, make something, etc.*).

4.1 Example

ACTIVITY 1   Study the following paragraph carefully. Underline the transition words and complete the analysis.

HOW TO SEARCH FOR INFORMATION ON THE INTERNET

In order to search effectively for information on the Internet, a person should choose the correct search engine, type in a narrow search topic, refine that search topic by further narrowing its scope, scan the descriptive entry under each website entry carefully, and read the website quickly, looking for the information needed. For example, imagine that information is needed about the climate of the small city of Sydney, Canada. First, choosing the correct search engine can facilitate the search because some search engines such as Hotbot, Snap!, LookSmart, and Dog Pound specialize in certain areas—and other search engines such as Lycos, Alta Vista, and Infoseek are best for general information. After choosing the search engine, next type in a narrowly focused search topic such as "Sydney, Canada." The computer will then produce a long list of websites, perhaps as many as 50,000 dealing with this subject. Next, before looking at any of these websites, further narrow the search by typing in more specific information such as "climate" or "weather." This will produce a more limited list of websites, usually less than 500. At this point, begin to scan the websites carefully. For example, a website entitled "Environmental Science Resources" may look initially promising—but closer examination will show it is a course taught at a university in Sydney. Usually, within the first group of ten websites, one website such as **http://www.ns.ec.gc.ca./weather** will appear; reading this website carefully, one can find an hourly update and a yearly review of all weather in Sydney, including temperature, humidity, barometric pressure, wind speed, rainfall, and cloud cover as well as other weather details. By following this process of identifying the correct search engine, narrowing the focus appropriately, and scanning and reading the websites carefully, the computer user can find relevant information quickly and efficiently.

Analysis

STEP 1: _____   EXAMPLE(S): _____

STEP 2: _____   EXAMPLE(S): _____

STEP 3: _____   EXAMPLE(S): _____

STEP 4: _____   EXAMPLE(S): _____

STEP 5: _____   EXAMPLE(S): _____

RESULT: _____

_____

4.2 Explanation

A process is a continuous series of steps that produces a result. A directional process analysis explains step-by-step how to do the process.

Directional process analysis does not emphasize *why* a person should do the process. Instead it answers the questions, *How do you do the process?* or *What are the steps in the process?*

In this type of paragraph, the sequence of steps is communicated as well as the steps themselves. Directional analysis paragraphs follow this pattern:

Title
Topic sentence
Step 1 Step 2 Step 3 (Other steps, if necessary)
Summary sentence

Preliminary Considerations

4.3 Choosing a limited subject

This paragraph should be about a process that needs human or animal help to be completed. It cannot be about a natural process that takes place automatically and without the help of directions. For example, "How Digestion Takes Place" is not a good subject for directional analysis since digestion is a natural process.

ACTIVITY 2   Which four of the following titles contain nonnatural processes as subjects? Put a check beside the correct answers.

How to Eat with Chopsticks   _____

How Does the Heart Pump Blood?   _____

How to Adjust a Canon AE-1 Camera   _____

How Is a Computer Programmed?   _____

How Photosynthesis Is Achieved   _____

How to Change a Baby's Diaper   _____

ACTIVITY 3   As always, your title must be very limited and specific. "How to Design a Suspension Bridge" is much too complex for only one paragraph. Write four limited titles for a directional analysis paragraph. Begin two titles with "How to" and make two titles questions.

_____

_____

_____

_____

4.4 Assessing relative importance

In any process there are numerous steps, some important, some moderately important, some extremely important. After you choose the process you will give directions for, you must decide which steps are the most important. Choose the steps carefully.

ACTIVITY 4   Imagine that the subject of your paragraph is "How to Impress a Person on a First Date." A preliminary list of steps in the process might look like the following list. Put a check beside the three steps you think are the most important.

1. Politely ask the person for a date.   _____

2. Call a good restaurant and make reservations.   _____

3. On date day, clean your car inside and out.   _____

4. Buy a flower for the date.   _____

5. Just before the date, take a shower.   _____

6. Put on some sweet perfume or cologne.   _____

7. Dress neatly and appropriately.   _____

8. Go to the place where the date lives exactly on time.   _____

9. Give the flower to the date.   _____

10. Compliment the date on his or her appearance.   _____

11. Take the date to the restaurant.   _____

12. Choose a dark romantic corner with candles
    and soft music.   _____

13. Eat slowly and try to have an interesting conversation.   _____

14. Afterward, drink coffee at the restaurant or go to a café.   _____

15. Be sensitive to the date; take the date home   _____
    whenever he or she wants to go.

Remember: *There are no right or wrong answers, but ask yourself which steps are less obvious and perhaps less important than others. Compare your answers with those of another student.*

ACTIVITY 5 *Look at the title below. Make a preliminary list of ten steps and then check the most important ones.*

HOW TO HAVE A GOOD PARTY

Preliminary list:

_____

_____

_____

_____

_____

_____

_____

_____

_____

_____

4.5 Getting the order right

After you have closely examined the process and determined the most important steps, you should make sure that you have exactly the right order. Even if only one step is in the wrong place, the entire process may not be accurate, and the reader may be misled.

ACTIVITY 6   *Put the sentences in the paragraph in the right order.*

HOW TO GET AN OKLAHOMA DRIVER'S LICENSE

If he can see well enough, he moves to the third test, the driving test. Now he can get his temporary license, and his permanent license will be sent to him within sixty days. This test uses an eye chart to measure the applicant's ability to see large and small objects at varying distances. When the applicant first goes to the Division of Motor Vehicles Office, he has to fill out an application form and pay a fee so that he can begin the written test. In order to get an Oklahoma driver's license, the prospective driver must complete the written exam, the eye test, and the driving test successfully. Finally, if he passes that test, he is ready for his photo to be taken. The written test consists of thirty-six multiple choice questions, such as:

The legal speed for a school zone in Oklahoma is:

    A. 40 mph   B. 15 mph   C. 20 mph   D. 25 mph

In this test, he drives around the city for fifteen to twenty minutes performing certain driving maneuvers, such as backing up and parking. To pass the written test, he must have no more than five errors. Second, after successfully passing the written test, the testee takes a standard eye test.

_____

_____

_____

_____

_____

_____

_____

_____

_____

_____

_____

_____

Writing the Directional Analysis Paragraph

4.6 The topic sentence

After you order the most important steps, you are ready to write the topic sentence. In the topic sentence of directional analysis paragraphs, the general idea is the process, and the specific parts are *short* descriptions of each step.

Example: To create a website at Geocities.com, a person

|_____ general idea _____|

must "homestead" a location, choose a user name and password, and use an editor to input website information.

|_____ specific parts _____|

ACTIVITY 7 *Write a topic sentence based on the information you compiled in Activity 6.*

_____

_____

_____

_____

_____

_____

_____

4.7 Language patterns in the subject development

The steps of the process must be clear and in the exact order. The subject development of directional analysis shows the continuous nature of these steps. Therefore, the following sequence transition patterns are often used:

A. Language pattern to show the object and its parts

STEP 1	STEP 2	STEP 3	LAST STEP
First	Second	Third	Finally
To begin with	After	Next	At last
Initially	Afterward	Then	
To start with	Next	Thereafter	
	Then	After	
	Thereafter	Afterward	

B. Sequence Pattern 2 to show one action that precedes another

$\begin{bmatrix} \text{After} \\ \text{When} \end{bmatrix}$ the noodles $\begin{bmatrix} \text{soften} \\ \text{have softened} \\ \text{have been softened} \end{bmatrix}$, remove them from heat.

After $\begin{bmatrix} \text{softening} \\ \text{having softened} \end{bmatrix}$ the noodles, remove them from the heat.

C. Sequence Pattern 3 to show two actions that happen at the same time

$\begin{bmatrix} \text{While} \\ \text{At the same time} \\ \text{As} \end{bmatrix}$ the sauce is heating, boil the noodles.

or

While heating the sauce, boil the noodles.

ACTIVITY 8   Complete the following paragraph by applying the language patterns. For practice do not use "first," "second," "third," "fourth"; it may be necessary to use a word more than once. Then complete the analysis.

HOW ARE SPICY CHINESE EGGS MADE?

Gathering the ingredients and equipment, boiling the eggs, scalding the beef, stewing the beef, and simmering the eggs and beef together are the necessary steps for cooking spicy Chinese eggs. _____ , gather these ingredients: ten large eggs, 2 pounds of round beef, 2 teaspoons each of salt, pepper, ginger, garlic, soy sauce, sesame oil, and green onion; a piece of star anise; 2 soupspoons of soy sauce. The equipment is two medium-sized pots and one big pot. _____ getting these materials, boil water in one of the medium pots and harden the eggs in it (about ten minutes). _____ the eggs are hardening, use the other medium-sized pot to scald the beef with boiling water. _____ the beef has boiled 2 or 3 minutes, remove it and wash the beef in cool water. At the same time, put the hot, hardened eggs into the cool water too, so they can be shelled easily. _____ the beef has been washed, strew it in the big pot, adding the teaspoons of ingredients mentioned in the first step and the piece of star anise. Heat the mixture on "low" for one hour. _____ , put the shelled eggs into the stewing beef, and add the two remaining soupspoons of soy sauce. _____ , "simmer" the beef and eggs together until a brown color appears on the eggs (about 1 hour). If these steps do not produce delicious eggs, go straight to a Chinese restaurant and let an expert prepare them for you!

Analysis

General process: _____					
STEP 1	**STEP 2**	**STEP 3**	**STEP 4**	**STEP 5**	**RESULT**
			Stewing the beef Add tsp. . . . Heat low 1 hour Add eggs/ soy sauce		

ACTIVITY 9 *FOOD TIME! Prepare a typical food from your country and bring it to class for an "International Meal Day" (either breakfast, lunch, or dinner). Write down the recipe for the food you bring since your class might like to compile a cookbook of all the recipes. Before, during, or after the meal, describe to the class how you made the food that you brought.*

4.8 The Summary Sentence

There are two similar kinds of summary sentence for directional analysis:

Method A: A summary sentence that contains a general reference to the *result* of the process

Example: If these steps do not produce *delicious eggs*, go straight to a Chinese restaurant and let an expert prepare them for you!

Method B: A summary sentence that gives the *specific results* of the process

Example: If the farmer follows these directions, he will obtain *high yields from his plants and not have weed problems.*

ACTIVITY 10   *The following paragraph does not have a summary sentence. Write two summary sentences for it, using Method A and Method B.*

HOW TO TELEPHONE SOMEONE OUTSIDE THE UNITED STATES

To make an international call station-to-station from the United States, a caller must dial the international access code, the country code, the city routing code, and the local telephone number. To start with, dial the international access code 011. This number is the same for every international call regardless of country. Next dial the country code. This code is a two- or three-digit number and can be obtained from the phone book in most cases. Afterward, dial the city routing code. This code is always a one- to five-digit number; it also can usually be obtained from the telephone book. Finally, dial the local number. If the number is needed, it can be obtained from operator assistance. For example, to place a telephone call to telephone number 123456 in Geneva, Switzerland, the following sequence would be dialed:

011	+	41	+	22	+	123456
International access		Switzerland code		Geneva code		local number

Summary sentence using *Method A*:

_____

_____

_____

Summary sentence using *Method B*:

_____

_____

_____

Stylistic Problems in Directional Analysis

4.9 Substitutes for the Conversational "You"

When writing English, the writer should avoid using the conversational "you" whenever possible. This is especially true in directional analysis in which the natural tendency is to write, "First, you should do this," or "First, you have to do this," or simply, "First, you do this."

The word "you" is very personal, but it is usually impossible for the writer to know the personal situation of the reader. Therefore, try to substitute a less personal, more formal word for "you."

Not good: In order to take a photograph, you must adjust the lens.

Better: In order to take a photograph, the photographer must adjust the lens.

or

In order to take a photograph, one must adjust the lens.

It is important to note that the imperative mood is frequently used in directions. In imperative sentences the subject is not written, but it is understood. Instead of using "your" as the following pronoun, try to replace it with "the."

Not good: You must buy the nails to complete *your* doghouse.

Better: Buy the nails to complete *the* doghouse.

ACTIVITY 11   Read the paragraph below. Change each of the italicized subjects and verbs to the imperative mood. Use the definite article "the" in place of the pronoun "your."

HOW TO USE THE LAUNDROMAT'S AUTOMATIC WASHER

To effectively use this washing machine, *you must complete* four steps carefully: loading the clothes, pouring in the detergent, adjusting the water temperature, and inserting the money. First, *you throw* clothes of similar color and fabric into the machine; for example, whites, colored clothes, and towels should be washed separately. While completing this step, *you must be* careful not to overload the machine, which normally has a capacity of about 2 kg. Second, *you should read* the directions on *your* detergent box to find out the correct amount for *your* particular load. For instance, with Tide detergent, *you dump* 1/2 cup in a front loading machine and 1 1/4 cups in a large capacity top-loader. Next, *you should select* one of three possible water temperatures: hot, warm, or cold. Generally, hot temperature is used for white clothes, warm temperature for permanent press, and cold temperature for dark or brightly colored clothes. Finally, after closing the machine's lid, or door, *you should insert* the proper amount of money in the slot. If the machine doesn't work, *you should try* inserting another coin or kicking the machine or both. In summary, by following these simple directions, the washer will get a clean load of wet clothes.

ACTIVITY 12   Read the paragraph again, substituting "the person who is washing" for "you" and "the" for "your."

Revision and Editing

4.10 Improving a paragraph

ACTIVITY 13 Evaluate the following two paragraphs about Japanese flower arranging. Then tell specifically why the first paragraph is better.

(1) HOW DOES THE SOUGETSU FLOWER ARRANGER WORK?

To arrange flowers according to the Sougetsu school, the arranger should choose a suitable flower bowl or vase, consider the flowers' position, then choose, cut, and arrange the flowers and branches. The flower arranger uses a *Kenzan* (flower bowl or vase), special flower scissors, water, seasonal flowers, and tree branches. For example, imagine that flowers are being prepared for the doll's festival (March 3). In this case, the flower arranger uses three peach tree branches with peach blossoms and five yellow narcissuses. First, choose a flower bowl with color and form to compliment the branches and flowers. Then choose the best narcissuses and peach tree branches because they will occupy the central position in the arrangement. Next the arranger should cut the flowers and branches according to his or her feeling and experience. Then the narcissuses and branches from the peach tree are arranged. Finally, if any problem occurs while arranging flowers, ask the teacher of flower arrangements for help.

(2) ARRANGING FLOWERS IN JAPAN

The process of arranging flowers according to a Japanese school of flower arranging takes five steps: choosing a flower vase or flower bowl, thinking about the position of the flowers, choosing flowers and branches, cutting flowers and branches, and arranging flowers and branches. The person arranging the flowers uses a flower vase or flower bowl called a *Kenzan*, special kinds of scissors for flowers, water, seasonal flowers, and some kind of tree branches. First, choose a flower vase or a flower bowl. The important point is its color and form. Next put water into the flower vase or flower bowl. Then choose the best flower and best branch because the best one has to be in the main position in the flower vase or flower bowl. Then cut them. This decision depends on the arranger's feeling and experience. Finally, if any problem happens while arranging the flowers, call the teacher and ask for help.

In the column marked "Reason," tell why each aspect of the first paragraph is better.

Analysis

ASPECT	REASON
1. Title	
2. Topic sentence	
3. Clear sequence	
4. Subject development	

4.11 Sentence correction

ACTIVITY 14 *Each sentence has one mistake. Find the mistake and correct it.*

1. First the man puts their arms around his partner's waist.

   Edited:

   _____

   _____

   _____

2. The applicant should go to the department and request an interview with graduate advisor.

   Edited:

   _____

   _____

   _____

3. After chosen a large pot, fill it with good soil.

   Edited:

   _____

   _____

   _____

4. The lotus position is not an easiest for beginners.

   Edited:

   _____

   _____

   _____

5. A few practice throws before throwing the frisbee to the dog.

   Edited:

   _____

   _____

   _____

6. Place the telescope in a high hill away from city lights.

   Edited:

   _____

   _____

   _____

7. While she is sitting beside the boy, she must smoothly turns the lights out.

   Edited:

   _____

   _____

   _____

8. To begin with, the writer thinks of a good topic sentence, then he develops his ideas in the subject development.

   Edited:

   _____

   _____

   _____

9. It is important for the player to look on the ball when it touches the racket.

   Edited:

   _____

   _____

   _____

10. To examine the quality of the cement, the mason must gather his equipment, mixing the cement blend, putting his cone into the blend, and process the experiment.

    Edited:

    _____

    _____

    _____

Application

4.12 Writing assignment

Write a paragraph in which you explain how to do something. Choose one of the following subjects, or a similar one of your own choosing.

Factual topics

1. How to perform a sports maneuver
   Examples: How to hit a baseball
   How to make a jumpshot in basketball
   How to kick a soccer ball
   How to swim the butterfly stroke

2. How to perform a personal maneuver
   Examples: How to kiss a boy or girl
   How to dance the _____ (name of dance)
   How to play the _____ (musical instrument)
   How to have a successful interview

3. How to operate some equipment or perform a scientific experiment
   Examples: How to operate a tractor
   How to use an electron microscope
   How to catalyze an enzyme
   How to prune a tree

4. How to cook a delicious food

Imaginative topic

1. How to cook a new food. Invent a new dessert, vegetable, or meat surprise!

2. How to _____
   (choose a funny subject and develop it imaginatively.)

Plan your paragraph carefully before you begin writing. (You might talk over your ideas with a classmate or with the class as a whole.) Then write a rough draft—revising as you write. When you have finished, share your writing with one or more students in your class. What do they think? Are there any points that they think are unclear? How can you better communicate your ideas?

Make any revisions that are desirable or necessary. Then edit your paragraph using Appendix B. Submit your final copy to your teacher.

Chapter 5

Cause Analysis and Effect Analysis

In this chapter, cause and effect paragraphs are described, with particular attention to organizational methods.

The Nature of Cause Analysis and Effect Analysis

5.1 Examples

5.2 Explanations

Preliminary Considerations

5.3 Choosing a limited subject

5.4 Assessing relative importance

5.5 Organizational methods

Writing Cause Analysis and Effect Analysis Paragraphs

5.6 The topic sentence

5.7 Using statistics in the subject development

5.8 Language patterns in the topic sentence and subject development

5.9 The summary sentence

Special Grammar in Cause Analysis and Effect Analysis

5.10 Review of the passive

Revision and Editing

5.11 Paragraph improvement

5.12 Sentence correction

Application

5.13 Writing assignment

The Nature of Cause Analysis and Effect Analysis

LET'S TALK ABOUT IT! With your small discussion group, consider each of the following items. Try to think of at least three effects of numbers 1–10, and at least three causes of numbers 11–18. During the discussion, when one member proposes a possible cause or effect, give your opinion and why you agree or disagree. Feel free to ask your group members to explain their opinions.

What would be the effect if:

1. everybody in the world were extremely thin? extremely fat?
2. watching TV were against the law?
3. you were very much in love with a person who didn't love you?
4. you had been born in the United States?
5. the existence of God were scientifically proven?
6. marijuana, cocaine, and heroin were legal?
7. you were extremely poor?
8. the most powerful country in the world were Brazil?
9. you woke up tomorrow morning and the whole world were covered with snow?
10. 1000 space ships from another planet in outer space landed on Earth?

What are some of the causes of:

11. poverty?
12. English being the international language?
13. Disneyland's and Disneyworld's success?
14. soccer's popularity?
15. elephants and gorillas nearly becoming extinct?
16. divorce?
17. increasing world population?
18. world problems?

FOLLOW-UP QUESTION   *All of the following items cause problems in the world. First, have each individual in the group rank them in importance. Then discuss them in your group and rank them again according to the consensus of the group.*

1 = most important   10 = least important

_____ environmental pollution

_____ overpopulation

_____ religious intolerance

_____ discrimination against women

_____ political differences between nations

_____ the gap between rich and poor nations

_____ racism

_____ starvation

_____ AIDS

_____ destruction of rainforests

5.1 *Examples*

ACTIVITY 1 *Study the following two paragraphs carefully and complete the analyses.*

DINKS IN ASIA

The low birth rate, which has been brought about by high prices and the changing social situation of women, is one of the most serious problems in Asia. When people talk about it, you can hear a word that was first coined in Japan, "DINKS," which means Double Income No Kids. First, in many major Asian cities such as Seoul, Hong Kong, Singapore, and Tokyo, the cost of a house is extremely high. A young couple who want to buy their own house may have to pay as much as $300,000 (even though real estate prices have been falling). In the case of an apartment which has one bedroom, one dining room, a kitchen, and a bathroom, the couple will have to pay approximately $900 a month. Moreover, if they want to have a child, the child's education is very expensive. For example, most kindergarten fees are at least $5000 a year. In such a situation, it's very difficult to afford children. Second and more importantly, the number of married women who want to continue working is increasing rapidly because these women enjoy their jobs. However, if they want to have children, they immediately have serious problems. Even though most companies have maternity leave, they expect pregnant women to quit their jobs. In short, if they want to bring up children properly, mothers and fathers both have to work, but it's very hard for mothers to work. Indeed, women who want to continue working have to choose between having children or keeping their jobs. In conclusion, Asian governments must take steps to alleviate the present situation as soon as they can.

Analysis

Effect: Low birthrate in Asia

Cause 1: _____	Cause 2: _____
Specific Information:	Specific Information:

HOW HUMANS CAN BENEFIT FROM TAKING VITAMIN A

Scientific studies have shown that vitamin A may have beneficial effects in clearing up skin problems, treating eye disorders, and fighting infection. Tablets with vitamin A have been used effectively in treating skin problems like acne. When applied directly on the skin, vitamin A can also clear up boils and heal ulcers. Injections of vitamin A have even been used to remove warts from people's skin. Vitamin A is a successful way of treating such eye disorders as night blindness and blurred vision. In addition, therapeutic doses of vitamin A are used to treat glaucoma and conjunctivitis (inflammation of the eyelids). Most important, vitamin A plays in integral role in fighting infections. Because it strengthens cell walls, vitamin A protects the mucous membrane from invading bacteria. Furthermore, dosages of vitamin A have shortened the duration of communicable diseases, such as cold and measles. In conclusion, these many beneficial effects demonstrate the importance of encouraging people to take regular dietary supplements of vitamin A.

Analysis

Cause: Use of Vitamin A in the body

Effect 1: _____	Effect 2: _____	Effect 3: _____
Examples:	Examples:	Examples:
_____	_____	_____
_____	_____	_____

5.2 Explanations

A. Cause analysis
   In a "cause" paragraph, the writer usually wants to discover the reason why a situation exists or the reasons why a change has occurred in a situation.

B. Effect analysis
   An effect is the result of a cause. An effect analysis paragraph explains the main effects that result from a cause.

   In effect analysis, the writer simply answers the question *What are the effects of this cause?*

   Each cause analysis and effect analysis paragraph should follow this pattern:

Title
Topic sentence
Cause A (or) Effect A   Cause B (or) Effect B   Cause C (or) Effect C   (Other causes or effects)
Summary sentence

Preliminary Considerations

5.3 *Choosing a limited subject*

Remember that you are writing a paragraph, not a book. Some subjects require extensive information in order to be properly developed. For example, "The Causes of Injuries in Sports" is a huge subject that many books have been written about. Similarly, "The Effect of Overpopulation in the World" is an appropriate subject for a book, not a paragraph.

Nonetheless, both of the above topics might be narrowed into appropriate subjects for a paragraph.

> *Too general:* The Effects of Overpopulation *in the World*
> *More specific:* The Effects of Overpopulation in Mexico City
> *Too general:* The Causes of Injuries in Sports
> *More specific:* The Causes of Knee Injuries in Tennis

ACTIVITY 2   *Narrow the following topics by making the italicized words more specific:*

1. *General:* The Causes of the Low *Crime* Rate *in Islamic Countries*

   Specific:

   _____

2. *General:* The Effects of *Music* on *People*

   Specific:

   _____

3. *General:* The Effects of *the Media* on *Society*

   Specific:

   _____

4. *General:* The Causes of *People's* Satisfaction with *the President*

   Specific:

   _____

5. *General:* The Effects of *Bad Weather* on *Plants*

   Specific:

   _____

5.4 Assessing relative importance

In directional analysis, the writer is faced with the problem of numerous steps; similarly, in cause analysis and effect analysis, he is faced with multiple causes or multiple effects. Often when a writer thinks deeply about a subject, he discovers numerous causes or effects. When this is true, the writer can use statistical evidence or personal experience to determine which causes or effects are most important.

ACTIVITY 3   *Use your personal experience to write down six possible causes and effects of "An Increase in the Average American's Weight." Then check the three causes and three effects you consider most important.*

A. Causes of "An Increase in the Average American's Weight"

    drinking more beer   _____

    _____   _____

    _____   _____

B. Effects of "An Increase in the Average American's Weight"

    _____   _____

    _____   _____

    _____   more heart problems

Discuss your choices with another student and explain how you assessed the importance of the causes and effects.

5.5 Organizational methods

The organization of causes or effects presents the writer with problems. *Which cause or effect will come first, second, third, etc., in the paragraph?* Three methods are frequently used to organize the causes or the effects.

1. *Importance method*

   First cause or effect = least important

   Last cause or effect = most important

   This method is used if the writer believes that the causes or effects vary in importance.

2. *Development method*

   First cause or effect = least developed

   Last cause or effect = most developed

   This method is used if the writer believes that the causes or effects are equal in importance, but the amount of information that the writer has varies in quantity.

3. *Logical method*

   First cause or effect = first in natural sequence

   Last cause or effect = last in natural sequence

   This method is used when some natural sequence, such as time or space, presents itself to the writer.

ACTIVITY 4   *Look back at the first example paragraph in this chapter. This paragraph uses the* Importance method.

How does the writer indicate which cause is the more important?

_____

_____

ACTIVITY 5   *Study the following paragraph. Determine which method is used and complete the analysis.*

WHAT CAUSES BICYCLE ACCIDENTS?

Most bike accidents are due to equipment failure, weather conditions, and biker carelessness. To begin with, many different pieces of bicycle equipment can become defective and cause bike accidents. For example, if a bike does not have good brakes, it cannot be stopped effectively. Similarly, a weak light will make it more difficult for a biker to see at night. Aside from defective equipment, a biker often has difficulty controlling his bicycle when it is windy and rainy. Under such conditions, water may impair the brakes and obstruct the biker's view; too much wind will affect steering. Nonetheless, bike accidents are mainly caused by biker carelessness. For example, accidents can be produced by a biker who does not stop at a stop sign and by a biker whose pants' legs get caught in the bike chain. The number of bike accidents could be greatly reduced if bikers checked their equipment, rode in good weather, and practiced bike safety.

Analysis

Cause A: _____	Cause B: _____	Cause C: _____
Example 1:	Example 1:	Example 1:
Example 2:	Example 2:	Example 2:

Result: Bicycle accidents

Writing Cause Analysis and Effect Analysis Paragraphs

5.6 The topic sentence

A. *Cause analysis*

In the topic sentence of a cause analysis paragraph, the general idea is the situation, and the specific parts are the causes.

Example: The decrease in energy consumption during the summer of 1998
⌞———————————— general idea ————————————⌟

was caused by an intensive advertising campaign, the cool summer, and high electricity prices.
⌞———————— specific parts ————————⌟

   ACTIVITY 6   Write a topic sentence based on the information in Section 5.4A.

_____

_____

B. *Effect analysis*

In the topic sentence of an effect analysis paragraph, the general idea is the cause, and the specific parts are the effects.

Example: Bad behavior, poor health, and wasted time are
⌞——————— specific parts ———————⌟

problems that result from children watching too much TV.
⌞———— general idea ————⌟

   ACTIVITY 7   Write a topic sentence based on the effects of smoking cigarettes.

_____

_____

5.7 Using statistics in the subject development

It is not necessary to use statistics in the subject development if the writer uses examples that are common knowledge, as, for example, in the "causes of bike accidents" paragraph. However, if the writer wants to develop causes or effects that are not common knowledge, statistical information should be used.

ACTIVITY 8   Read the following paragraph. Imagine that you are a Colombian, and that your audience is a group of Americans. What statistical information would help you communicate your idea more effectively?

WHY CRIME IS INCREASING IN COLOMBIA

Inflation and lack of job opportunities are the main factors that have produced an increase in the crime rate of Colombia. Inflation is a big problem in Colombia because many people who work don't make enough money to live or to educate their children. Also the lack of job opportunities is another main cause of increasing crime. Unemployed people have no way to get food or even a place to live because the government does not provide any social services for the poor. In conclusion, the government must stabilize the currency and build factories to employ the people so that the crime rate will drop.

Rewrite the paragraph so that it includes at least four pieces of information from the following statistics:

Major crimes (murder, robbery, assault) have increased 185 percent since 1997.

By 2000 there were two million unemployed Colombians (8 percent of the population).

A good education costs 6,000 Colombian pesos ($120US) per month per child; only middle- and upper-income children attend school.

The average Colombian makes a salary of about 13,000 pesos per month ($250US).

The inflation rate in 1990 was 14 percent; the rate by 2000, 26 percent.

Eighty percent of Colombia's unemployed live in the streets of towns and cities.

The average Colombian family has an income of 18,000 pesos per month ($360US); of this $350US is spent for survival (food, clothing, shelter).

Fifty-five percent of all major crimes are committed by unemployed people.

Twenty-five percent of all major crimes are committed by workers who make less than 13,00 pesos a month.

Rewrite the paragraph.

WHY CRIME IS INCREASING IN COLOMBIA

_____

_____

_____

_____

_____

_____

_____

_____

_____

_____

_____

_____

_____

_____

5.8 Language patterns in the topic sentence and subject development

The topic sentence and subject development of a cause analysis and effect analysis paragraph show how causes produce an effect or how effects are produced by a cause. Therefore, the following language patterns are used:

A. Pattern 1 to show the causes that produce an effect

CAUSES		EFFECT
Drug use and unemployment	cause produce bring about	crime.
Drug use and inflation occur,	producing bringing about causing	crime.

(or)

EFFECT		CAUSES
Crime	is caused by is produced by results from is brought about by	drug use.
Crime occurs mainly	as a result of because of due to	drug use.

B. Other patterns in cause and effect analysis

If unemployment produces crime, *then* jobs must be found.		
Because Since	unemployment produces crime, jobs must be found.	
Unemployment produces crime;	accordingly, therefore, consequently, for this reason, thus,	jobs must be found.

ACTIVITY 9   *Use the language patterns on page 104 to complete the following paragraph.*

MAJOR CAUSES OF JOGGING FOOT INJURIES

Joggers get foot injuries mainly _____ unequal leg length, weak feet, and improper training. About 15 percent of all runners have unequal leg length. In such runners, the ankle and foot often rotate abnormally _____ muscle strain on the foot. Next, surveys indicate that 35 to 65 percent of all runners have weak feet. _____ the feet are weak, _____ the force of the feet hitting the ground _____ abnormal strain on the muscles of the foot. _____ a jogger's foot hits the ground about 1,000 times during every ten-minute mile, the result for a weak-footed jogger is muscular or skeletal damage to the feet. Finally, improper training often _____ major foot problems. For example, sudden changes in the duration or frequency of runs place added stress on the feet. Similarly, changing from running on dirt to running on pavement greatly increases muscular strain inside the feet; _____ , well-made running shoes should be bought to cushion the feet and reduce strain on them.*

5.9 The Summary Sentence

There is one main method of writing summary sentences for cause analysis and effect analysis paragraphs.

Main method: Ways to stop the causes or effects or to continue them.

Example: The number of bike accidents could be greatly reduced if bikers checked their equipment, rode in good weather, and practiced bike safety.

Example: In conclusion, these many beneficial effects demonstrate the importance of encouraging people to take regular dietary supplements of vitamin A.

* Bob Glover and Jack Shepard, *The Runner's Handbook* (New York: Penguin, 1977)

ACTIVITY 10   The paragraph in Activity 10 does not have a summary sentence. Write a summary sentence for it in which you suggest a way of alleviating the causes of foot injuries in general.

<u>Joggers could lessen the number of foot injuries by</u> _____

_____

_____

ACTIVITY 11   Small group discussion. Your task is to design the perfect English program. Imagine that you are the directors of a small English program of about 25 students. You want to increase your student population and, at the same time, offer the highest quality of instruction possible. At present you have only two classrooms and no language laboratory. You have four teachers and one secretary.

When discussing the points on the following page, try to consider the effects of your decisions. Also try to use the language patterns listed in Section 5.8.

Answer the following questions:

1. The university has provided you with a budget of $250,000 for the upcoming year. What percent (how many dollars) will you spend on each of the following items?

   building two new classrooms   _____

   salaries for three new teachers   _____

   general operating expenses (electricity, etc.)   _____

   creating a language laboratory   _____

   providing food machines in a student lounge   _____

   hiring a new administrative staff person
   to help with housing and visas   _____

General points:

STUDENTS

2. How many students do you *eventually* want to have in your program?
3. Should you try to limit the number of students from any one country? If no, why not? If yes, what should be the maximum number?
4. How many students should be in each class?

CLASSES

5. How many classes per day should each student take?

6. What hours of the day should the students study?

7. How long should each class be? 50 minutes? one and a half hours? two hours? three hours? different classes with different lengths?

8. How many and how long should student breaks be? lunch break?

9. Should the program offer any electives? What electives should be offered?

_____

_____

_____

10. What subjects should the students study, in what order, and at what times? Fill in the grid below.

Time	*Class*
_____	_____
_____	_____
_____	_____
_____	_____
_____	_____
_____	_____

STUDENT AMENITIES

11. Put these amenities in order of importance to you.

    1 = most important   5 = least important

    free coffee and doughnuts   _____

    a student library   _____

    video/VCR facilities for students   _____

    free parking   _____

    student copy machine   _____

Special Grammar in Cause Analysis and Effect Analysis

5.10 *Review of the passive*

ACTIVITY 12   Review the form of the passive that was presented in Section 3.9. After reading the following paragraph, rewrite the italicized phrases in the passive tense below.

MAJOR CAUSES OF JOGGING FOOT INJURIES

[1]*Joggers incur foot injuries* mainly as a result of unequal leg length, weak feet, and improper training. About 15 percent of all runners have unequal leg length. In such runners, [2]*abnormal rotation of the ankle and foot often produces muscular strain in the foot.* Next, surveys indicate that 35 to 65 percent of all runners have weak feet. If the feet are weak, then [3]*the force of the feet striking the ground causes abnormal strain on the muscles of the foot.* Since a jogger's foot hits the ground about 1,000 times during every ten-minute mile, the result for a weak-footed jogger is muscular or skeletal damage to the feet. Finally, [4]*improper training often produces major foot problems.* For example, [5]*sudden changes in the duration or frequency of runs place added stress on the feet.* Similarly, [6]*changing from running on dirt to running on paved surfaces greatly increases muscular strain inside the feet;* [7]*runners should buy well-made running shoes* to cushion the feet and reduce strain on them.

1. _____

_____

_____

2. _____

_____

_____

3. _____

_____

_____

4. _____
   _____
   _____

5. _____
   _____
   _____

6. _____
   _____
   _____

7. _____
   _____
   _____

Revision and Editing

5.11 *Paragraph Improvement*

ACTIVITY 13 *Read the following rough draft carefully. Then, after answering the questions below, revise the draft.*

WHAT ARE THE EFFECTS OF ALCOHOL?

Financial, social, and health problems can all result from a person drinking too much alcohol over a long period of time. Habitually drinking a large quantity of alcohol can be very costly.

AMOUNT OF ALCOHOL BOUGHT PER WEEK	WEEKLY COST	YEARLY COST	THIRTY-YEAR COST (NO INFLATION)
2 6-packs of beer	$ 8.00	$ 416.00	$12,480.00
2 6-packs of beer, 1 gallon of wine, 1 fifth of whiskey	$30.00	$1,560.00	$46,800.00

Other hidden costs include more expensive car and medical insurance. The extra medical insurance is necessary because alcohol damages important parts of the body. For example, medical reports show that alcohol kills brain cells, weakens the heart, burns holes in the stomach, and destroys the liver. In the last case, alcohol reduces the liver's ability to produce red blood cells, leading directly to cirrhosis and ultimately to death. As if killing themselves is not enough, alcoholics also have a terrible effect on society. Society and its citizens could be greatly improved if alcohol were consumed moderately or not at all!

1. What is the problem regarding the topic sentence and the organization of the subject development?

_____

_____

_____

2. How is the point about social impact incomplete?

_____

_____

_____

3. Rewrite the point about social impact. Add one example to show the effect of alcohol on business, and one example to show the effect of alcohol on families. Try to find some statistics about alcohol in a book, world almanac, or encyclopedia. (*Add only two sentences.*)

_____

_____

_____

_____

_____

_____

_____

_____

_____

_____

5.12 Sentence correction

ACTIVITY 14 Each sentence has one mistake. Find and correct the mistake.

1. If a boy visits a girl in her house, the girl's parents leaves the house.

   Edited:

   _____

   _____

   _____

2. TV which is watched an average of five hours a day by children who rarely read books anymore.

   Edited:

   _____

   _____

   _____

3. For example, 60 percent of the children that watch TV have weak vision they must wear glasses from an early age.

   Edited:

   _____

   _____

   _____

4. Drug use is increasing because of influence of foreign workers.

   Edited:

   _____

   _____

   _____

5. Many opportunities for recreation has a person when he spends his time outside.

   Edited:

   _____

   _____

   _____

6. Chinese women live an average of seventy-eight years but Chinese men have a life expectancy of only seventy-one years.

   Edited:

   _____

   _____

   _____

7. Each man receives their driver's license at age seventeen.

   Edited:

   _____

   _____

   _____

8. The decrease in poverty is direct result of industrialization.

   Edited:

   _____

   _____

   _____

9. Poor parenting is one cause of teenage drug use and of teenage girls getting pregnant.

   Edited:

   _____

   _____

   _____

10. The university system is one of the biggest reason.

    Edited:

    _____

    _____

    _____

Application

5.13 Writing assignment

Write one cause analysis and one effect analysis paragraph. When you write the paragraphs, you must use statistics from at least one reference: a book, magazine, newspaper, world almanac, or encyclopedia. Be sure to give the exact name of the reference you use.

Plan your paragraphs carefully before you begin writing. Then write a rough draft, revising as you write. After finishing your rough draft, join a group of at least two other students. Using Appendix B, the members of the group should evaluate each other's paragraphs. Then, members should discuss their evaluations and exchange ideas. Finally, each member of the group should rewrite his or her paragraphs and turn them in to the teacher, along with the other students' evaluations of the paragraphs.

Cause Analysis

1. Write a paragraph in which you develop two or three causes of an increasing social problem in your country, such as crime, divorce, drug use, poverty, traffic accidents, decline in religion, or worker laziness.

2. Write a paragraph in which you describe two or three causes of an improving situation in your country, such as reduced inflation, reduced unemployment, better housing, lowered birth rate, or longer life expectancy.

3. Write a paragraph in which you discuss and explain the causes of a political problem in your part of the world, such as in Central America, Southeast Asia, or the Middle East. Be careful to use facts, not unsupported personal opinion. Try to be objective and brief.

Effect Analysis

1. Write a paragraph in which you describe the good or bad effects of a substance, such as a vitamin or drug, on the human body. Include at least three effects and be as scientific as possible.

2. Write a paragraph in which you develop at least three effects of TV on society.

3. Write a paragraph in which you give at least three good or bad effects—or a combination of both—that a recent political leader has had on your country.

Imaginative cause analysis

Write a paragraph about the causes of something you believe will happen in the distant future. For example: *People will live underground, people will begin using horses for transportation again, insects will take over a part of the world,* or *people will travel to other planets on space ships as easily as we take airplane trips around the world today.*

Imaginative effect analysis

Imagine that some incredible event happens in the future. For example: *Life is found on other planets, the existence of God is proven scientifically,* or *disease is wiped from the face of the earth.* Write a paragraph about the effects of such a momentous event.

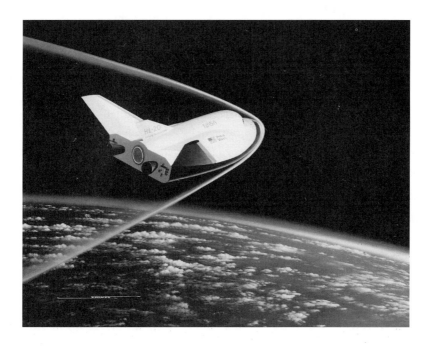

Chapter 6

Explanation by Comparison and Contrast

This chapter describes the comparison and contrast paragraph, examining the two methods of organizing such paragraphs.

The Nature of Comparison and Contrast

LET'S TALK ABOUT IT! *Below is a list of fifteen topics for discussion. Pretend you are at a party. Stand up and walk around your class discussing with each class member at least five of the topics for comparison and contrast. Go slowly and attempt to make a conversation based on each of your classmates' answers. Be sure that your classmates give you at least one similarity and one difference for each question. Do not stop until you have talked to everyone in your class.*

Note: *if your class has more than fifteen people, you may be able to ask only three or four questions of each person.*

Please compare and contrast:

1. dogs and cats
2. your language and English
3. Coke® and Pepsi®
4. a shower and a bath
5. your mother and your father
6. your home city and the city we're in now
7. newspapers and magazines
8. your two favorite musicians
9. your grammar class and your vocabulary class
10. your life now and your life in twenty years
11. your best friend and yourself
12. tennis and basketball
13. riding in a car and riding in an airplane
14. summer and winter
15. love and hate

This "party" discussion may be followed by a full class discussion of the same fifteen topics.

6.1 Example

ACTIVITY 1   *Read the following paragraph. Complete the analysis.*

WHAT ARE SOME POINTS TO CONSIDER WHEN CHOOSING BETWEEN A BMW 320I AND A HONDA CIVIC?

The German-built BMW 320i and the Japanese Honda Civic offer interesting points of similarity and difference to the prospective car buyer in the areas of length/weight, interior size, and engine capacity. The BMW 320i is considerably longer and heavier than the Civic. The BMW measures 178 inches long and weighs 2,500 pounds. On the other hand, the Civic is only 161 inches long with a weight of 2,000 pounds. Nevertheless, the BMW and the Civic have surprisingly similar interior dimensions:*

	BMW 320I	HONDA CIVIC
Overall width	63 inches	62 inches
Door, top to ground	60 inches	48 inches
Maximum front leg room	41 inches	41 inches
Rear, fore-aft seat room	26 inches	24 inches

Perhaps the most significant difference between the two cars is the engine volume and net horsepower. With a 108 cubic inch volume and a maximum 101 horsepower (6800 rpm), the BMW is substantially different from the Civic, whose engine has only 91 cubic inches with a maximum of 67 horsepower (5000 rpm).* To summarize, the car buyer should consider these points (as well as the obvious price difference) when deciding which of these cars to buy.

* *Consumer Reports, 1987*

Analysis

General subject:	BMW 320i/Honda Civic	
Reason for paragraph:		
Basis of Comparison and Contrast	Specific Characteristics or Examples	Similarity or Difference
1. _____	_____	_____
2. _____	width: 62/63 legroom 41/41 door: 50/48 rear 26/24	similarity
3. _____	_____	_____

6.2 Explanations

If a writer analyzes two subjects carefully, he or she usually discovers that they have similarities (*points of comparison*) and differences (*points of contrast*). For this reason, a comparison and contrast paragraph communicates the important similarities and differences between two subjects.

For example, if a writer writes a paragraph emphasizing the similarities between two subjects, he or she must also discuss at least one difference, and visa versa.

All comparison and contrast paragraphs follow one of the two patterns discussed later in this chapter.

Preliminary Considerations

6.3 Focusing on the title

Comparison and contrast should be used to show some fact or facts: *Who was the best player? Which is the worst car? What is the most difficult language?*

For example, we can focus on the title "A BMW 320i and a Honda Civic" by directing the paragraph toward people considering buying one of those cars: "Which Car Is Best for a Student, a BMW 320i or a Honda Civic?"

ACTIVITY 2   *Change the following titles into more clearly focused ones.*

1. The Nile and the Amazon

_____

_____

2. A Tiger and a Lion

_____

_____

3. Communism and Capitalism

_____

_____

4. Celine Dion and Mariah Carey

_____

_____

6.4 Thinking deeply about the subject

To write comparison and contrast effectively, you must think deeply about your two subjects. Try to think of significant similarities and differences. For example, if your subjects are a tiger and a lion, do not state the obvious and write that they are both animals, or if you are writing about a Mercedes and a Nissan, do not waste space by writing that they are both cars.

ACTIVITY 3   *Write down the significant similarities and differences between each pair of subjects listed below.*

A. _____ your language _____ / ___ English _____

Similarities

1. _____

2. _____

Differences

1. _____

2. _____

3. _____

B. _____ tennis _____ / ___ soccer _____

Similarities

1. rectangular playing field _____

2. _____

Differences

1. _____

2. _____

C. (you choose) _____ and _____

Similarities

1. _____

2. _____

Differences

1. _____

2. _____

Writing Comparison and Contrast Paragraphs

6.5 The topic sentence

After you have thought deeply about the subject and chosen two or three significant similarities and differences, you can write the topic sentence. In this sentence, the general idea is the two subjects of the comparison and contrast; the specific parts are the bases of comparison and contrast—the similarities and differences.

Example: Representation, coloring, and appeal are bases for
└——————————— specific parts ————————————┘

comparing and contrasting the paintings of
Picasso and Cezanne.
└——————————— general idea ———————————┘

ACTIVITY 4   *Read the following paragraph; then write a title and a topic sentence for it.*

_____

_____

_____

_____

Although these two rhythms are Colombian, they have a foreign origin. The "cumbia" was created by African slaves who were brought to the hot Caribbean regions of the country to work in the gold mines. It was a sad song of these people who wished for escape and for their families. In contrast, the "bambuco" has a white, Spanish origin. It was created in colder zones where the Spanish wanted to express love to their girlfriends. The cumbia is mainly played with two instruments, the flute and the drum (male and female), while the bambuco is only played with the guitar. Despite its sad beginnings, the cumbia has become a happy rhythm that people dance to with enthusiasm at parties and carnivals, such as the Barranquilla carnival. On the other hand, the bambuco remains a sad and soft rhythm that people sing to express love for their lovers, to congratulate another person on a special day, or to express sorrow for a mistake. Even though the cumbia and bambuco are different rhythms, both of them today are composed by humble blacks and whites to show their common feelings and emotions. In summary, this final similarity explains the universality of music and the reason the cumbia and bambuco have not been replaced by modern rhythms.

6.6 *Two methods of comparison and contrast organization*

In a comparison and contrast paragraph, there are two main ways to organize the subject development.

Method 1: A comparison and contrast of Subject 1 and Subject 2

A. Subject 1
    1. Point of comparison or contrast
    2. Point of comparison or contrast
    3. Point of comparison or contrast
B. Subject 2
    1. Point of comparison or contrast
    2. Point of comparison or contrast
    3. Point of comparison or contrast

Method 2: A comparison and contrast of Subject 1 and Subject 2

A. Point of comparison and contrast
    1. Subject 1
    2. Subject 2
B. Point of comparison and contrast
    1. Subject 1
    2. Subject 2
C. Point of comparison and contrast
    1. Subject 1
    2. Subject 2

ACTIVITY 5   *Fill in the outline of the paragraph in Section 6.5 to show that you understand its organization.*

A. _____

    1. _____

    2. _____

B. _____

    1. _____

    2. _____

C. _____

    1. _____

    2. _____

D. _____

    1. _____

    2. _____

ACTIVITY 6 *Study the following paragraph carefully. Which method of organization is used? In the space after the paragraph, rewrite it using the other method.*

THE CHANGING FACE OF SAUDI ARABIA: SHAGRA AND RIYADH

To see how Saudi Arabia is changing, the old town of Shagra (population 30,000) and the modern capital of Riyadh (9,000,000) can be analyzed with respect to physical characteristics, commerce, residential environment, and citizens' religious activities. First, the narrow unpaved streets of Shagra contain no traffic lights or signs, and are lined with mud houses and shops. Some of Shagra's commercial activities, such as the buying and selling of cloth, take place in the small, hot shops; however, most basic transactions, such as camel and horse trading, occur outside in the town marketplace. Since most of the town's residents live and work in the same small area (5 x 5 km²), everyone knows everyone else; the rich man helps the poor man, and the young man helps the old man. In doing this, Shagrans are fulfilling the meaning of Islam—that all men are brothers—a meaning that has remained unchanged for centuries, like Shagra herself. Unlike Shagra, the developing city of Riyadh has numerous asphalt highways that connect the governmental and industrial workers' concrete homes in the suburbs with the multistoried business offices downtown. In fact, most of Riyadh's business decisions are made in air-conditioned conference rooms, just as its residents shop for cloth and food in air-conditioned department stores and supermarkets. Because most workers commute over a large area (45 x 45 km²), few of them have the time to make friends or help their neighbors. Nonetheless, the spirit of Islam pervades the city; daily prayer calls are constantly heard, and the rule against doing business on holy days is strictly enforced. This brief look at Shagra and Riyadh clearly shows the transition state in which Saudi Arabia finds herself.

Rewrite the paragraph using the *other* method.

_____

_____

_____

_____

_____

_____

_____

_____

_____

_____

_____

_____

_____

_____

_____

_____

_____

_____

_____

_____

_____

_____

6.7 Language patterns in the subject development

The subject development of a comparison and contrast paragraph emphasizes the similarities and differences between the two subjects under discussion. Therefore, the following patterns are often used.

A. Pattern to show contrast

Most mammals don't lay eggs;	in contrast, conversely, on the other hand, however, on the contrary,	all reptiles do.

B. Patterns to show contrast

Kuwait is	different from unlike	Egypt in regard to oil supply.

(*or*)

Different from Unlike	Egypt, Kuwait has large supplies of oil.

C. Patterns to show concession

Even though Although Despite the fact that In spite of the fact that (While) (Whereas)	the TV show is good, the movie is better.

(*or*)

The TV show is good;	nonetheless, nevertheless,	the movie is better.

D. Pattern to show similarities

Korea's Green Island is beautiful;	similarly, likewise, in the same way,	Brazil's Island of St. Sebastian is extremely scenic.

ACTIVITY 7   *Complete the following paragraph by applying the language patterns; then do the analysis.*

WHO WAS THE BETTER BASKETBALL PLAYER, CHAMBERLAIN OR RUSSELL?

A brief study of Russell's and Chamberlain's scoring, rebounding, defensive, and leadership abilities will show which one was the better player. Career offensive statistics reveal a considerable difference:

	Games Played	Total Points	Average
Russell	963	14,522	15.1
Chamberlain	1,045	31,419	30.1

Russell was a fairly good scorer; _____, Chamberlain was the greatest offensive star in NBA history (even scoring 100 points in one game!). Insofar as rebounding is concerned, Russell averaged 21.4 a game and had 51 in one game; _____, Chamberlain had 21.8 rebounds a game and had 55 in one game. Although the league keeps no defensive statistics, Russell is commonly acknowledged by sports fans and sports magazines as "the greatest defensive player ever." Opposing teams were forced to change their plans and opposing centers lost sleep when they had to face Russell. _____, Chamberlain was considered lazy on defense because he preferred to concentrate so much on offense. From a leadership standpoint, Russell led his team, the Boston Celtics, to eleven World Championships in thirteen years, and he was the league MVP five times. _____, Chamberlain played for three teams in fourteen years and won the MVP four times; his teams won the championship twice.

Analysis

General subject: _____

Reason for paragraph: _____

Bases	Specific Details	Similarity or Difference
1. _____	_____	_____
2. _____	_____	_____
3. _____	_____	_____
4. _____	_____	_____

6.8 The summary sentence

There are two main types of summary sentences in comparison and contrast paragraphs.

> *Type 1:* A summary sentence that presents a conclusion based on the information given.

> *Example:* In summary, this final similarity explains the universality of music and the reason the cumbia and bambuco have not been replaced by modern music.

> *Type 2:* A summary sentence that restates the purpose of comparison and contrast.

> *Example:* This brief look at Shagra and Riyadh clearly shows the transition state in which Saudi Arabia finds herself.

ACTIVITY 8   *Change the summary sentence of the paragraph about Saudi Arabia to a Type 1 summary sentence.*

Are these changes good for Saudi Arabia? In conclusion, _____

_____

Write a summary sentence of Type 1 for the paragraph about Russell and Chamberlain.

Based on this information, we can conclude that _____

_____

Special Grammar in Comparison and Contrast

6.9 Using relative clauses

Relative clauses are often used to change two sentences into one sentence. Study how this is done in the following examples.

Example 1: Russell led his team to eleven World Championships. He was the best player in the league five times.

Russell (he was the best player in the league five times) led his team to eleven World Championships.

Russell, *who was the best player in the league five times,* led his team to eleven World Championships.

In Example 1, the relative pronoun replaces the subject of the second sentence; when this happens, the relative clause has this construction:

relative clause = relative pronoun + verb + compliment

Example 2: The new machines have arrived. The company bought the new machines.

The new machines (the company bought the new machines) have arrived.

The new machines *that the company bought* have arrived.

In Example 2, the relative pronoun replaces the object of the second sentence; when this happens, the relative clause usually has this construction:

relative clause = relative pronoun + subject + verb (compliment)

In both examples the relative clause is placed just after the noun it modifies. The main relative pronouns used in writing are:

who—refers only to persons
which—refers only to things
that—refers to person or things
whose—refers to persons or things

ACTIVITY 9 *Change each pair of sentences into one sentence by replacing the second sentence with a relative clause as directed.*

1. The BMW is longer and heavier than the Civic. The BMW measures 178 inches long and weighs 2500 pounds.
   Replace the subject of the second sentence with a relative pronoun.

   _____

   _____

   _____

2. The cumbia was created by African slaves. The African slaves were brought to work in the gold mines.
   Replace the subject of the second sentence with a relative pronoun.

   _____

   _____

   _____

3. The BMW is different from the Civic. The Civic's engine has only 91 cubic inches.
   Replace the first two words of the second sentence with a possessive relative pronoun.

   _____

   _____

   _____

4. The cumbia has evolved into a cheery rhythm. The people dance the cumbia with a lot of enthusiasm.
   Replace the object of the second sentence.

   _____

   _____

   _____

5. Water polo is a physically demanding sport. Swimmers play water polo only after long conditioning programs.
   Replace the object of the second sentence.

   _____

   _____

   _____

6. The manufacturing plant gives bonuses every year. The manufacturing plant makes pipelines for oil companies.
   Replace the subject of the second sentence.

   _____

   _____

   _____

7. AT&T provides operator-assisted long distance service. Business people prefer AT&T's long distance service to that of other companies.
   Replace the object of the second sentence.

   _____

   _____

   _____

8. The thumb functions differently from the forefinger. The forefinger's nail can be used for cleaning the fur.
   Replace the first two words of the second sentence with a possessive relative pronoun.

   _____

   _____

   _____

   Punctuation note: Commas are needed before and after the clauses in sentences 1 through 4 because these clauses are nonrestrictive, that is, they are not essential. Sentence 6 contains a restrictive clause; therefore no commas should be used to set off the clause. How should the other sentences be punctuated?

ACTIVITY 10   Study the following paragraph. Change each italicized sentence into a relative clause and include it in the sentence that comes before it.

WHERE DO YOU WANT TO SKI?

California's cross-country ski resorts of Rock Creek and Royal Gorge can be analyzed with respect to lodge life, trails, and prices. Skiers at Rock Creek relax by a fire in the small, primitive lodge, drink beer, and eat country food in the tiny cookhouse. *Rock Creek is located near Bishop in the eastern Sierras.* On the other hand, Royal Gorge is near Lake Tahoe in the western Sierras; its two-story lodge has a big fireplace, warm carpeting, and overstuffed furniture. *The lodge was built in 1921.* Royal Gorge also has a French chef. *His cooking is eaten by the light of oil lanterns.* Second, most of the skiing at Rock Creek is back-country skiing through mountains; there are only 20 kilometers of groomed trails. Conversely, Royal Gorge does not offer back-country adventure, but it has 225 kilometers of groomed trails. *These trails are constantly patrolled in case a skier needs help.* Pricewise, these two Nordic resorts are similar: a three-day weekend costs $110 at Rock Creek and $130 at Royal Gorge, per skier. In summary, if you are looking for a primitive back-country experience, ski at Rock Creek; if you want French cooking and easy trails, head for Royal Gorge.

1. _____

_____

2. _____

_____

3. _____

_____

4. _____

_____

Revision and Editing

6.10 Paragraph improvement

ACTIVITY 11   Read the following final draft, and evaluate it as directed.

PICASSO AND CEZANNE

The representation, coloring, and appeal of the paintings of Picasso and Cezanne can be analyzed to help us better understand their works. First, I can say a most different point is their expression. They used quite different methods of painting their artistic spirit. Picasso was cubist, and Cezanne was an impressionist. Cubists try to represent all forms by using cubes and rectangles, whereas impressionists try to represent all objects using personal impression. Second, for the reason above, Picasso's paintings were made with black and primary colors—red, blue, and yellow, whereas Cezanne's paintings were drawn from white and other colors. They are so beautiful. Third, Picasso's paintings appeal to us as strongly as Cezanne's paintings. They take masses of all their objects. In conclusion, Picasso and Cezanne have the support of many people despite their obvious differences.

Give the paragraph a grade based on the following:

Content

1. Does the writer show deep knowledge of the subject?

_____

2. Does the writer include good examples (the names of paintings) in the subject development?

_____

Organization

3. Does the writer have a clear, directed title?

_____

4. Does the writer have a good topic sentence?

_____

5. Does the writer follow the same order in the topic sentence and subject development?

_____

6. Does the writer have a good summary sentence?

_____

General good and bad points:

_____

_____

_____

_____

_____

_____

_____

Grade for the paragraph (A, B, or C) _____

6.11 Sentence correction

ACTIVITY 12 Find and correct the mistake in each sentence.

1. The *Gulag Archipelago* and *Moby-Dick* are about good and evil and written by Solzhenitsyn and Melville.

   Edited:

   _____

   _____

   _____

2. Kihajau Dewan was a teacher who he had studied in the Netherlands.

   Edited:

   _____

   _____

   _____

3. Of all rose colors, the red rose is the more popular.

   Edited:

   _____

   _____

   _____

4. *2001* is a best science fiction movie ever made.

   Edited:

   _____

   _____

   _____

5. Nureyev who left the Soviet Union whose interpretation of *Swan Lake* was overwhelming.

   Edited:

   _____

   _____

   _____

6. The Datsun 210 station wagon gets good gas mileage, it has poor acceleration.

Edited:

_____

_____

_____

7. The platypus is the only egg-layed mammal.

Edited:

_____

_____

_____

8. This two types of sunglasses are popular.

Edited:

_____

_____

_____

9. The Thai educational system places the most emphasis in group performance.

Edited:

_____

_____

_____

10. Many of Rembrandt's paintings is located in the Rijksmuseum in Amsterdam.

Edited:

_____

_____

_____

ACTIVITY 13 In a small group, consider the following questions. Throughout the discussion, focus on the ways in which animals and humans are alike and different.

1. Are humans animals? Explain.
2. Do you consider yourself an animal? If no, why not? If yes, why?
3. How are animals different than humans? Consider various animals such as worms, birds, monkeys, etc.
4. Which animals do you consider the most intelligent? Name at least three.
5. Which animals do you consider the least intelligent? Name at least three.
6. a. Do you have or have you ever had a pet? Describe the pet.
   b. Can (or could) you communicate with your pet? Describe how.
7. a. In general, do you feel any connection to animals? For example, do you feel "bad" when you read or hear that elephants, whales, and other species are being killed to the point of extinction? Explain.
   b. Similarly, have you ever eaten a dog? a cat? a fly?
   c. What is the difference between eating a cat and eating a cow?
8. a. How do you feel about using animals for medical experiments? Explain.
   b. Is it acceptable to use humans, prisoners for example, in medical experiments?
9. Is there any difference between killing an animal in an experiment and killing an animal for food?
10. Some countries such as Sweden have recently passed laws protecting animals. How do you feel about such laws? Are they necessary? Explain.

Application

6.12 Writing assignment

Write a comparison and contrast paragraph. Plan your paragraph carefully. Before you begin writing, you might talk over your ideas with a classmate or with the class as a whole. Then write a rough draft, revising as you write. When you have finished, share your writing with one or more students in your class. *What do they think? Are there any points that they think are unclear? How can you better communicate your ideas?*

Make any revisions that are desirable or necessary. Then edit your paragraph using Appendix B. Submit your final copy to your teacher.

Choose one of the following subjects.

Factual

1. Write a paragraph comparing and contrasting two artists (painters, musicians, writers, dancers).
2. Write a paragraph comparing and contrasting a system (educational, political, social) in two countries.
3. Write a paragraph comparing and contrasting two animals of the same order (mammals, reptiles) or two plants of the same family.
4. Write a comparison and contrast paragraph of two competing products, such as Coke and Pepsi or Big Macs and Burger King Whoppers.
5. Write a paragraph about two movies, books, or TV shows. (Approve the title with your teacher before writing.)
6. Write a paragraph based on your discussion in Activity 14.

Imaginative

Write a paragraph in which you compare and contrast two fictional politicians who want to be president of your country. Describe which one would be best.

Chapter 7

Persuading by Argument

This chapter analyzes the elements of an argument, with emphasis on the importance of refutation.

The Nature of Argument

Preliminary Considerations

Writing the Argumentative Paragraph

Special Grammar in Argument

Revision and Editing

Application

The Nature of Argument

LET'S TALK ABOUT IT! *With one or more of your classmates, have a long conversation in which you carefully consider the following ideas. In your conversation, give two reasons to support and two reasons not to support each idea.*

1. People should be allowed to carry guns.
2. Abortion should be legal.
3. The world would be better if all world leaders were women.
4. Governments should not support religion.
5. We should create a new world with no countries.
6. Marijuana should be illegal.
7. People under thirty should not be permitted to marry.
8. The government should not give money to help poor people.
9. Chinese should become the new international language.
10. The death penalty is a good punishment for murderers.
11. It is usually more difficult for a man to work at a job (outside the house) than for a woman to work at jobs inside the house.
12. Humans are basically good.

After these conversations with your classmates, you will consider some of these subjects with the whole class, so try to remember what is said during your conversations.

7.1 Example

ACTIVITY 1   *Read and analyze the following paragraph carefully.*

ARE FEMALES BIOLOGICALLY STRONGER THAN MALES?

Greater life expectancy rates and lower death rates indicate that women may be biologically "stronger" than men. It is common knowledge that in almost every country (industrialized or developing), the life expectancy of women at birth exceeds that of men.

LIFE EXPECTANCY AT BIRTH (2000)[*]

Country	Male	Female
Chad	31	37.3
China	62	68.7
Japan	76.4	84.6
Norway	77.1	82.1
Peru	54.8	60.5
Saudi Arabia	48.5	53.9
The United States	70.4	79.2
Russia	65	77

Yet these statistics alone are not persuasive. In fact, people who believe that men are biologically stronger than women (or at least as strong as) claim that women live longer because men work harder and are exposed to more stress and danger in their jobs. This idea can be refuted by looking at death rate statistics. Even though the number of male and female births are roughly the same (slightly more females), more males die in every age group, from fetus to ninety years old. For example, United Nations statistics show that in the United States in the period 1946–1948, fifteen boy babies in the first year of life died for every ten girl babies that died. Certainly these boy babies did not work harder or have more stressful and dangerous lives than the girl babies. During the same years, at age fifty-five, the ratio was almost the same: eighteen men died for every ten women.[*] Considered together, life expectancy rates and death rates strongly suggest that women are biologically stronger than men.

[*] *United Nations Statistical Yearbook* (1998) "Projections for the Year 2000."

Analysis

Proposal: _____

_____

Point of support (reason for): _____

Examples (choose two): _____

_____

Opponent's argument (reason against): _____

_____

Refutation of opponent's argument: _____

_____

7.2 Explanation

In an argument, the writer tries either to change the way the reader thinks or to influence the reader to do something. Generally, the writer wants the reader to:

1. accept or reject an idea
2. realize that action should be taken to solve a problem
3. try a new way of doing something

To persuade the reader, the writer gives information (evidence) to support his or her viewpoint. Then the writer considers the best argument against his or her viewpoint that an opponent might have, and tries to refute that argument by showing why it is wrong, weak, or of lesser importance.

The process of an argument can be summarized as follow:

proposal = (writer's ideas + evidence)
  reasons for
    + (opponent's argument + refutation + evidence)
        reasons against

Preliminary Considerations

7.3 A proposal worth arguing

The title of an argumentative paragraph states or suggest the writer's idea—the proposal. An argument is not normally a place for neutrality. The writer has formed an idea and wants the reader to form the same idea. If the writer wants to change or influence the reader, the writer must demonstrate the *necessity* of reading the writer's proposal.

In other words, the writer should avoid obvious proposals. Imagine that the title of the model paragraph had been "Are There Biological Differences Between Males and Females?" Would it have been necessary for you to read the paragraph?

ACTIVITY 2   Read the following proposals. Which ones are the least obvious?

1. Space exploration should be stopped.
2. Was Picasso a great painter?
3. Automobile pollution in Los Angeles is a major problem.
4. Aerobic exercise is not good for women.
5. Young children should not be allowed to eat too much sugar.
6. Americans love money.
7. Life in the Sahara desert is difficult.
8. Should Chinese women with more than one child be sterilized?

Remember, as always, that you are writing a paragraph, and that your proposal should be narrowed to a manageable focus.

7.4 *The reasons for and reasons against*

After you have a clear idea about your proposal, make a list of at least three reasons (pros) in support of your proposal and the main reason (con) *against* your proposal. Imagine that you propose "All Handgun Sales Should be Prohibited." You might come up with the following reasons for and against:

REASONS FOR (PROS)
would decrease violent crimes
would save taxpayer money
  (fewer police)
would help create a better
  social environment

REASON AGAINST (CON)
would restrict individual
  freedom (a person couldn't
  buy what he or she wanted)

ACTIVITY 3   *Write three reasons for and one main reason against each of the following proposals.*

1. *Proposal:* Prostitution should not be legalized.
   Reasons for:

   _____

   _____

   _____

   *Reason against:*_____

2. *Proposal:* Religion and government should be separate.
   Reasons for:

   _____

   _____

   _____

   *Reason against:*_____

3. *Proposal:* The world would be better with one language.
   Reasons for:

   _____

   _____

   _____

   *Reason against:*_____

7.5 *The refutation*

Now that you have thought deeply about your proposal, considering the reasons for and the main reason against, you must think even more deeply. You must attack and refute the opponent's main reason against the proposal. There are three basic methods of attacking and refuting your opponent's main reason against the proposal.

Method 1: Demonstrate that your opponent's reason is wrong because it is based on incorrect or misleading information.

Method 2: Show that your opponent's reason is weak because it is based on insufficient information or ignores significant information.

Method 3: Agree that your opponent's reason is valid, but show that your points of support are more compelling.

Look back at Section 7.4. In "All Handgun Sales Should be Prohibited," you might respond to the reason against in the following way:

MAIN REASON AGAINST
would restrict individual freedom (a person couldn't buy what he or she wanted)

ATTACK AND REFUTATION
Method 2: The opponent is partially right—freedom to buy would be restricted, but freedom from fear and freedom of movement would be increased.

ACTIVITY 4   *Look back at Activity 3. How would you respond to each of the reasons against listed there?*

1. *Proposal:* Prostitution should not be legalized.
   Main reason against:

   _____

   Attack and refutation:

   _____

   _____

   _____

2. *Proposal:* Religion and government should be separate.
   Main reason against:

   _____

   Attack and refutation:

   _____

   _____

   _____

3. *Proposal:* The world would be better with one language.
   Main reason against:

   _____

   Attack and refutation:

   _____

   _____

   _____

ACTIVITY 5   *Study the following refutations. Which methods do they use? Note that these are merely* refutations *and not complete paragraphs.*

1. *Proposal:* Workers should not be forced to retire at age sixty-five.
   Main reason against and refutation:

Those who disagree with this proposal point out that as people grow older their bodies begin to slow down, and it is risky for them to continue working. Actually, this is true in only one respect—the body does slow down. However, accident rates for those over sixty-five are slightly less than those for people under sixty-five. How can we explain this? Simply, workers over sixty-five have far more experience in their jobs than younger workers, and workers over sixty-five are far more aware of their own limitations.

Method _____

_____

_____

2. *Proposal:* Abortion should be legal.
   Main reason against and refutation:

"Pro-life" people argue that abortion is the killing of a potential human being. This is undeniably true. Nevertheless, as has been pointed out, if abortion is illegal, there will be (1) a dramatic increase in unwanted, neglected, and abused children; (2) the number of women who die getting illegal, unhygienic abortions will increase greatly; and (3) women will lose what they have fought so hard for—the basic right to control their own bodies. These three points outweigh the argument of the pro-lifers.

Method _____

_____

_____

3. *Proposal:* Sex education is appropriate for sixth graders in the United States.

   Main reason against and refutation:

   The opponents of this idea claim that most eleven-year-olds have not seen information about sex; therefore, teaching them sex education would put the idea of sex into their minds. Nothing could be further from the truth; most eleven-year-olds have been exposed to sex long before the sixth grade. For example, the January 1998 Neilsen TV rating showed that two of the show most heavily watched by eight- and ten-year-olds were "Seinfeld" and "Friends"—both of which contain a heavy dose of sexual content. These and other TV shows, combined with drugstore sex magazines, "R"-rated movies, and even "sexy" comic books, expose children to sex long before they are in the sixth grade.

   Method _____

   _____

   _____

   ACTIVITY 6   Prepare the following flow chart for the proposal "Eighteen-year-olds are old enough to get married."

   Reasons for:

   _____

   _____

   _____

   Main reason against:

   _____

   Attack and refutation of the main reason against:

   _____

   _____

   _____

   Remember: *It is a good idea to prepare a flow chart before you begin to write an argumentative paragraph.*

Writing the Argumentative Paragraph

7.6 *The topic sentence*

In the topic sentence of an argumentative paragraph, the general subject is the proposal, and the specific parts are either the reasons for, or the refutation of the main reason against. For example, study the following topic sentences:

Example: Greater life expectancy rates and ⌐ lower death rates
└————— reason for —————┘   └refutation of main reason against —┘
indicate that women may be biologically "stronger" than men.
└——————————————— proposal ———————————————┘

All handgun sales should be prohibited because
└——————————— proposal ———————————┘
violent crime would decrease and
└——————— reason for ———————┘
the social environment would improve.
└——————— reason for ———————┘

ACTIVITY 7   Write topic sentences for the proposals you thought about in Activities 4 and 5.

1. _____

_____

_____

2. _____

_____

_____

3. _____

_____

_____

7.7 Evidence in the subject development

When you are developing your reasons for, and refuting the main reason against, you need to use appropriate evidence. There are three major types of evidence.

1. Statistical evidence or information based on research
2. Information based on personal experience and common sense
3. Information that compares similar things

ACTIVITY 8 Read the following information about killing whales, and tell whether it is Type 1, 2, 3, or a combination of these types. As you read the information, think about how it might be used to support the proposal "The Killing of Whales Should Be Stopped."

1. Whales are intelligent creatures that share our world. They are capable of communicating even to the point of composing whale songs. They are highly civilized, social creatures that maintain closely knit family groups. Killing such intelligent, civilized creatures is murder.
2. Whaling countries such as Japan and Russia do not need the whaling industry to support their economies. In fact, money from whaling represents only .00001% of the Japanese economy and .0002% of the Russian economy.
3. Buffalo, elephants, and rhinoceroses are other large mammals that have been driven to the point of extinction by man's killing.
4. The only way to stop the killing is to have laws against it; hunters will not stop voluntarily.
5. The Cousteau Society estimates that the number of whales has declined by 95 percent in the last 100 years. Moreover, if the slaughter continues at its present rate, the society believes that whales will become extinct in another twenty-five years.
6. It is cheaper to produce synthetic "whale" oil than to obtain natural oil from dead whales. Each kilogram of synthetic oil costs about $8.00 to produce, whereas it costs over $15.00 to obtain the same amount of natural whale oil.

7. Results of the moratorium on whale hunting in the north Atlantic, 1990–1997:

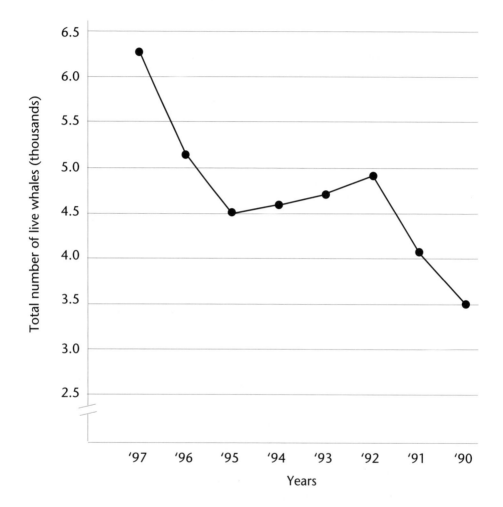

ACTIVITY 9   *Use some of the information from Activity 9 to complete the following paragraph.*

STOP THE SLAUGHTER OF WHALES!

The killing of whales must be stopped both for humanitarian and economic reasons. To begin with, whales are not a lower form of animal. _____

_____

_____

_____.

Moreover, technology has now advanced to the point that it is no longer necessary or economically feasible to kill whales for whale oil.

_____

_____

_____.

Nonetheless, opponents of this proposal claim that whaling industries constitute an important segment of the economy of whaling countries. This is obviously not true. _____

_____

_____

_____.

In summary, some action must be taken now. _____

_____

_____.

Help stop the killing of whales!

7.8 Some problems with evidence and logic

Writers of argument must be especially careful to avoid mistakes of evidence and logic. Three of the most common errors include:

False conclusion: The conclusion is not based on evidence.

Misplaced causes and effects: Just because one thing takes place before another doesn't mean it causes it; similarly, just because one thing follows another doesn't mean it is an effect of it.

Bad evidence: Evidence is used that comes from an outdated, incompetent, or biased source.

ACTIVITY 10   *Study the following "reasons for." What problems does each have?*

Reason 1:
There is no doubt that Serbian troops have been withdrawn from Kosovo. According to information released by the Serbian Interior Ministry, 87 percent of all troops had exited the Kosovo enclave as of the date required by the United Nations.

Problem:

_____

Reason 2:
Treating teeth with fluoride causes cancer. A research study, which tracked children who had had their teeth treated with fluoride, found that at age sixty, 7 percent of them had gotten cancer.

Problem:

_____

Reason 3:
The voting age in the United States should be lowered from eighteen to seventeen. At age seventeen, young people are allowed to drive unrestrictedly in twenty-five states and even drink alcohol in one (Arizona). If they drive and can drink alcohol, seventeen-year-olds should surely be able to vote.

Problem:

_____

7.9 Language patterns in the argumentative paragraph

A. Possible pattern to make a proposal in the topic sentence

I	propose urge recommend insist	that	the killing of whales	be	stopped because . . .
				(base verb)	

B. Pattern to cite a source or statistics

According to Based on	information from the United States government . . .

C. Patterns to introduce the main reason against

The opponents of Those who disagree with	this proposal	(might) (would)	argue assert declare claim say take the position	that . . .

D. Possible patterns to summarize

It is	essential important necessary vital urgent	that the killing of whales be stopped.

ACTIVITY 11   Read and analyze the following paragraph. Fill in the blanks, using the patterns on page 155 to communicate the ideas.

NO MORE ENGLISH

_____ English stop being used as the international language because it is symbolic of an exploitive colonial past, and is spoken by so few people in the world. The spread of English as a second language—or as the international language—began in the 16th century and has continued to the present time as a direct result of British and American colonialism. India, Malaysia, Singapore, and the Philippines are all examples of countries that have had English exploitatively forced upon them. By exploitatively, I mean that language is a critical component of the formation and maintenance of culture among people. A people's way of thinking and habitual behavior, which are parts of culture, are transmitted by language. To force a population to learn another language is to corrupt insidiously their way of thinking and habitual behavior—their culture. Ultimately, of course, the culture of the colonizer will take the place of the native culture. _____ proposal _____ English is already the international language of science, business, and popular conversation. This is at least partially true; scientists and business people do use English, but there are relatively few people _____ in the world who use English conversationally. _____ recent statistics, English is not spoken by more than 3.5 billion of the world's population. To put it in a different way, fewer than one out of ten people in the world speak English, and the proportion of English speakers is declining. In summary, _____ _____ the international language not be English.

Analysis

Proposal: _____

_____

Reasons for: _____

Examples: _____

_____

Reasons against (opponent's argument): _____

_____

Refutation of opponent's argument: _____

_____

_____

7.10 The summary sentence

The summary sentence in an argumentative paragraph should emphatically restate the proposal, stressing the necessity of accepting it. Below are the summary sentences you have seen thus far in this chapter.

1. Considered together, life expectancy rates and death rates strongly suggest that women are biologically "stronger" than men.
2. Help stop the killing of whales!
3. In summary, it is important that the international language not be English.

ACTIVITY 12 *Look back at Activity 8. Based on the topic sentences you wrote, compose three summary sentences for the same paragraphs.*

1. _____

_____

2. _____

_____

3. _____

_____

Special Grammar in Argument

7.11 *Noun clauses*

Noun clauses appear frequently in argument. There are many words that may introduce a noun clause, such as *whether, if, who, what, which, when, where, why* or *how*, but the most common introductory word is *that*. Noun clauses normally have the form:

that + subject + verb (+ compliment)

Noun clauses can function in any way that a noun can function. Four of the most common ways are:

1. as a subject
   That a nuclear war might end the world is undeniable.

2. as a subject after *it*
   It is undeniable *that a nuclear war might end the world.*

3. as an object of a verb
   Many scientists have written *that a nuclear war might end the world.*

4. as an appositive
   There is no question *that a nuclear war might end the world.*

ACTIVITY 13   *Change each pair of sentences into one sentence containing a noun clause. Then insert the sentence into the paragraph that follows. The sentences are not in the same order as they should appear in the paragraph.*

1. I think. It is asinine of him to spend his pocket money on cigarettes.
   (an object of a verb)

   _____

   _____

2. Many smokers have died of lung cancer. Everyone knows.
   (a subject—make the second sentence passive)

   _____

   _____

3. It is important. We remove cigarettes from all areas by law.
   (a subject after it*)*

   _____

   _____

4. There is a theory. Breathing air containing cigarette smoke is worse than smoking itself.
   (an appositive)

   _____

   _____

5. My opponents say. Smoking quiets their mental excitement and has an effect on dieting.
   (an object of a verb)

   _____

   _____

6. There is no doubt. Smoking does more harm than good in the long run.
   (an appositive)

   _____

   _____

MAKE CIGARETTES ILLEGAL

Smoking should be illegal because it harms good health, wastes money, and often causes fires. People are seldom seen smoking in the United States; in Indonesia, people smoke everywhere: in the office, at school, on the train. Smoking causes diseases. _____

_____.

_____

Also, _____

_____.

Second, most heavy smokers spend more than thirty dollars a month to buy cigarettes. If the smoker is a worker, this may not be a big expense, but if he is a student, _____

_____

Third, as a matter of fact, many accidents are caused by people smoking in bed who forget to extinguish their cigarettes. _____

_____.

These opinions may be true; however, _____

_____.

_____

_____.

ACTIVITY 14   *The first part of this activity should be performed outside the class if possible. Ask three people who are not in your class what they would do in the following situations. Afterward, in class, compare the answers you received with those received by one of your classmates. As you discuss the results, consider what you would do and try to think of reasons both for and against your decision.*

Situation 1: You are walking down a street in the United States and you see a $100 bill on the sidewalk. What would you do? Would you act the same if it were a $1,000 bill? What if it were a sidewalk in your country? What if you found a wallet with $10,000 in it?

Situation 2: You are shopping in a supermarket and you see a student stealing food. What would you do?

Situation 3: You are in the middle of a final exam and an acquaintance whispers that she wants to cheat off your paper. What would you do? What if she were your best friend?

Situation 4: You are at a party and you hear a racist joke. What would you do?

Situation 5: Your brother has been selling cocaine for several months. Two of his customers died last week from overdoses. What would you do?

Situation 6: You are walking down a street alone at 1 AM. You see a group of five men beating up an old man. He is screaming for help. What would you do?

Situation 7: You are a soldier—a private—in the army. After entering an enemy town, your commander orders you to enter an elementary school and shoot two children. He says that if you do not do it, you will be shot. What would you do? What if it were twenty children? 200? 2,000?

Revision and Editing

7.12 Paragraph improvement

ACTIVITY 15 *Read the following rough draft. Analyze it critically by answering the questions that follow.*

SOCIALIZED VERSUS PRIVATELY FINANCED HEALTH CARE

Socialized health care systems generally do not make sense. First, socialized medicine is extremely expensive—no matter how it is paid for. For example, in Sweden and Saudi Arabia, two medically socialized countries, the costs have increased to approximately 40 percent of the budget of each country per year. In Sweden, this money comes from high taxes; in Saudi Arabia, it comes from petrodollars. More than this, the socialized system is inefficient. Often it is hard to find an appropriate doctor, and it is even harder to be examined by a doctor. According to one recent case in Algeria, a woman had to wait eight months just to have her tooth filled. In countries with socialized medicine, everyone wants to go to the doctor or dentist no matter how small the problem might be. The opponents of this position argue that socialized medicine gives all the people a chance for health care (not only the rich). This is, of course, true, but we might ask, "What quality of health care does it give a chance for?" According to the American Medical Association, doctors in medically socialized countries generally possess less skill than those doctors in countries with privately financed health care. Simply speaking, if a doctor has a guaranteed supply of patients, what incentive (other than self-satisfaction) does the doctor have to improve his skills?

1. The topic sentence is incomplete; write a better one.

_____

_____

_____

2. Is the first *reason for* a good one? Is it reasonable to think about cost as a drawback to socialized medicine?

_____

_____

_____

3. In the *reason for* about inefficiency, does the one example justify the generalization?

_____

_____

_____

4. The writer quotes the American Medical Association; do you see any problem with this?

_____

_____

_____

5. Write a summary sentence.

_____

_____

_____

7.13 Sentence correction

ACTIVITY 16   Correct each of the following sentences.

1. Intensive suntanning wrinkles the skin and the chance of skin cancer is increased.

   Edited:

   _____

   _____

   _____

2. If cigarette companies are allowed to advertise in television, the number of young smokers will increase.

   Edited:

   _____

   _____

   _____

3. There are many evidences that the universe could have begun with a "big bang."

   Edited:

   _____

   _____

   _____

4. Millions of people had died in religions wars in the past.

   Edited:

   _____

   _____

   _____

5. Is abortion an only alternative for teenage girls?

   Edited:

   _____

   _____

   _____

6. Neither increased conservation in the wild nor more breeding in zoos are going to save the African elephant from extinction.

   Edited:

   _____

   _____

   _____

7. That prostitution is "immoral" is an opinion not disputing by most Venezuelan people.

   Edited:

   _____

   _____

   _____

8. Because of higher housing costs, increased crime, and lower government subsidies.

   Edited:

   _____

   _____

   _____

9. Experimentation on animals is not only barbaric as well as unnecessary.

   Edited:

   _____

   _____

   _____

10. Einstein recommended that nuclear energy must be tightly controlled.

    Edited:

    _____

    _____

    _____

Application

7.14 Writing assignment

Plan your paragraph carefully. Before you begin writing, you might talk over your ideas with a classmate or with the class as a whole. Then write a rough draft, revising as you write. When you have finished, share your writing with one or more students in your class. What do they think? Are there any points that they think are unclear? How can you better communicate your ideas?

Make any revisions that are desirable or necessary. Then edit your paragraph using Appendix B. Submit your final copy to your teacher.

Choose one of the following subjects.

Factual

1. Write an argument in which you propose an idea that will improve your country.
2. Write an argument in which you try to influence a person to act.
3. Choose one of the following subjects: *abortion, gun control, marijuana usage, internet censorship.* Write an argument for or against a particular viewpoint.

Imaginative

1. Write an argument in which you predict what country will be the most powerful in 1,000 years.
2. Write an argument supporting a proposal that you do not personally believe in. Your paragraph can be lighthearted or serious.

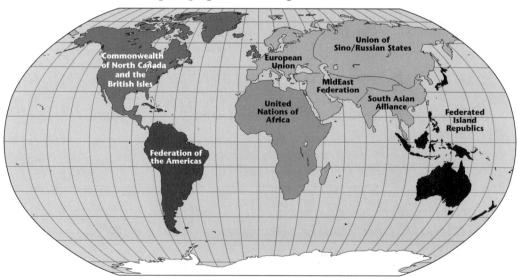

Map of Possible Countries of the World in the Year 3,000 AD

Chapter 8

Paragraph Practice

Paragraph 1   *Explanation by Definition*

DIRECTIONS   Write a paragraph defining a scientific or humanistic term.

WHAT IS ANTHROPOLOGY?

Anthropology is the study of man (from the Greek *anthropos* [man] and *logia* [study]). Unlike such sciences as zoology and botany, anthropology is concerned primarily with one species: *Homo sapiens*, or "Man the wise." Other sciences such as psychology or sociology also focus on the study of humanity; nonetheless, anthropological research is rather narrowly defined into two areas: physical anthropology and cultural anthropology. Physical anthropologists study human evolution from primates, focusing on fossil records, comparative anatomical studies of living primates, and observation of the social behavior of apes and monkeys. Moreover, physical anthropologists are interested in human variation, especially as it relates to blood chemistry and genetic development. While physical anthropology deals with the physical characteristics of human beings, cultural anthropology deals with what humans have produced; it can be subdivided into linguistics, archaeology, and ethnology. Linguistics is, of course, the study of language; archaeology is the study of extinct cultures; and ethnology is the study of living cultures—including such areas as religion, folklore, and art. In short, the goal of anthropology is to learn how humans have developed into their present condition and what their potentialities are for the future.

ACTIVITY 1 *Complete this analysis of the "Anthropology" paragraph.*

Term: _____

General definition: _____

_____

DIVISIONS

A. _____ B. _____

Goal: _____ Goal: _____

Focus: 1.   Subdivisions: 1.

      2.   2.

      3.   3.

EXPLANATION

In the topic sentence, the general idea is the term to be defined. The specific parts are the class and distinguishing characteristic(s) of the term being defined.

The subject development elaborates on the distinguishing characteristics of the term being defined. In other words, it describes what the term includes and how the term may differ from other closely related, or similar, terms.

In the summary sentence, the writer should restate the opening definition in light of what has been written in the subject development.

Paragraph 2 *Explanation by Cause and Effect*

DIRECTIONS   *Write a paragraph describing a cause and effect sequence in nature, in the laboratory, or in history.*

DDT DISASTER: PELICANS IN CALIFORNIA

The California brown pelican population was severely reduced in the 1950s and 1960s by a cause and effect cycle involving the insecticide DDT (*d*ichloro-*d*iphenyl-*t*richloroethane). In the 1950s, California farmers began using aerial spraying of DDT to kill insects infesting their crops. However, after the insecticide had accomplished its purpose, it did not disappear from the environment. Instead the DDT remained on the ground until it was washed into nearby lakes and rivers by seasonal rains. Once in the water, the DDT was absorbed by tiny marine plants and animals. Some of these organisms died; others were eaten by fish. The fish absorbed the DDT into their bodies; again some died, but others survived and were eaten by brown pelicans. The pelicans were not directly killed by the insecticide; however, the DDT made the shells of the pelican eggs so thin that they cracked easily. As a result, few baby pelicans were hatched. Between 1950 and 1972 (when DDT was banned), the brown pelican population in California declined from 2,500 to less than 500.

ACTIVITY 2 Complete the table giving the sequence in the "DDT" paragraph.

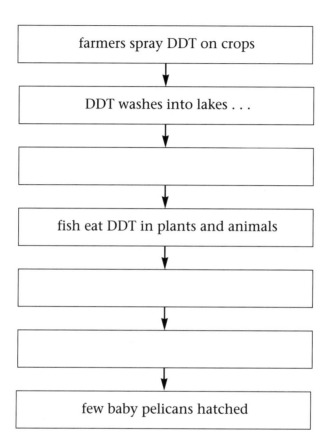

farmers spray DDT on crops
↓
DDT washes into lakes . . .
↓
↓
fish eat DDT in plants and animals
↓
↓
↓
few baby pelicans hatched

EXPLANATION

Earlier in this book you wrote a cause and/or effect paragraph. This paragraph differs substantially in that it requires you to describe a sequence in which each step is both a cause and an effect. Each step in cause *and* effect is directly caused by the preceding step.

The general subject of the topic sentence is the last effect; the specific part contains a reference to the basic characteristics of the sequence.

The subject development must be clear. The interconnections must be precise.

The summary sentence elaborates on the ultimate effect of the sequence.

Paragraph 3 *Explanation by Classification*

DIRECTIONS *Write a paragraph classifying a group of things in your major field of study or in a major interest that you have.*

RUNNERS

The jogger, the runner, and the marathoner can be easily distinguished by the clothing that each wears. To begin with, the jogger only runs once or twice a week around the block (usually between TV programs). The jogger always wears nonwhite socks and tennis shoes and usually covers his or her fat stomach with cut-off jeans and a white t-shirt. The daily runner, however, is much trendier with his or her clothes. Usually he or she wears the number-one rated shoes in *Running World* magazine (Nike or Reebok) and the newest synthetic shorts—designed to absorb the maximum amount of perspiration. The daily runner's T-shirt usually carries a slogan or brand name such as OP or Adidas. The ultimate runner, nonetheless, is the marathoner, who averages between 75 and 150 miles a week in twice-a-day workouts. This runner has transcended the running "shoes" worn by mere mortals to reach the stage of racing "flats." Usually the marathoner's shorts are the sheerest nylon briefs imaginable (to cut down air resistance), and his or her shirt was earned at a prestigious marathon (preferably Boston). The marathoner (who will occasionally disguise him- or herself as a jogger or runner in order to stun these slower runners when he or she swishes them off the road) loves to outrun bicycles, cars, and other forms of vulgar transportation. The next time you are riding in your car, see how many joggers, runner, and marathoners you can detect.

ACTIVITY 3 Complete this analysis of the "Runners" paragraph.

General class:

Subclass 1: Characteristics 1. 2. 3.	Subclass 2: Characteristics 1. 2. 3.	Subclass 3: Characteristics 1. 2. 3.

EXPLANATION

To classify means to group together individuals, ideas, or subjects that have shared characteristics. When classifying, the writer determines the basis of the classification. For example, apples can be classified by color:

green apples   yellow apples   red apples

Only one basis of division may be used at each level of classification. For example, if you are classifying apples by color, you cannot have:

green apples   yellow apples   sweet red apples

Also, each class must be mutually exclusive. In other words, if you are classifying runners by frequency of running, you cannot have

daily joggers   daily runners   twice-daily marathoners

In the topic sentence of a classification paragraph, the general idea refers to the general class and basis of classification; the specific aspects are the specific subclasses.

In the subject development, accurate description is extremely important to differentiate between classes. Organization is not a problem because each subclass has equal value.

The summary sentence of a classification paragraph generally tells why it is important to classify the subject.

Paragraph 4   *Explanation by Natural Process*

DIRECTIONS   *Write a paragraph describing a complex natural process.*

PHOTOSYNTHESIS

Photosynthesis is the essential process by which green plants capture light energy and use it to change water, carbon dioxide, and minerals into oxygen and high-energy organic compounds. A simple formula for this process might look like:

$$6CO_2 + 12H_2O \xrightarrow[\text{chlorophyll}]{\text{light}} C_6H_{12}O_6 + 6O_2 + 6H_2O$$

carbon dioxide   water   glucose   oxygen   water

For example, assume that there is a healthy spinach plant growing in the air (.04% CO_2) at $25°C$ and that this spinach has 1 kg of wet tissue containing 1 g of chlorophyll in its chloroplast. Sunlight hits this wet tissue; the light energy is captured or absorbed by the plant's chlorophyll. This energy is then transferred between the parts of the plant's chloroplast, ultimately being converted into chemical energy. In this light reaction, the bonds of the water molecule are broken (oxidation), and the carbon dioxide is reduced, forming oxygen, transferring hydrogen, and storing the chemical energy in the energy-rich molecule ATP (adenosine triphosphate). In fact, if the amount of light, CO_2, and temperature remain constant, the spinach plant will produce several liters of oxygen per hour. Moreover, in a subsequent dark reaction, the CO_2 is reduced, forming water, and the ATP assists in the production of carbon-rich compounds such as glucose, thereby completing photosynthesis.*

* *Encyclopedia Britannica* (Chicago: University of Chicago Press, 1998).

ACTIVITY 4 Complete this analysis of the "Photosynthesis" paragraph.

Phase 1: _____ Sunlight hits green plants _____ ⎤
_____ ⎟
Phase 2: _____ ⎟
_____ ⎟
Phase 3: _____ energy transferred / converted _____ ⎬ Result of process
_____ ⎟
Phase 4: ___ light reaction; bonds broken: oxygen / hydrogen / ATP ___ ⎟
_____ ⎟
Phase 5: _____ ⎦

EXPLANATION

The differences between directional process and natural process are mostly ones of style. For example, the imperative is obviously not used. On the other hand, other characteristics are similar, including clear sequence of steps and careful description of each step.

The topic sentence names the process and briefly describes its steps.

The subject development elaborates on each step of the process.

The summary sentence gives the result of the process.

Paragraph 5   *Neutral Argument*

DIRECTIONS   *Write a paragraph in which you discuss the reasons for and the reasons against a controversial issue—without taking a stand.*

DEATH PENALTY, YES OR NO?

In Switzerland, the death penalty doesn't exist because the majority of the population argues that miscarriage(s) of justice cannot be avoided; moreover, it might be harder to live behind bars for life than to be killed. Also, every person should have a chance at rehabilitation. Thus, even though he or she has committed an injustice, he or she should have the possibility of starting over again in another life-style. In opposition there are supporters of the death penalty with arguments like, Why do we have to subsidize terrorists in prison with our taxes? Why should there be a reason to bring the whole population in danger with blackmail and be assassinated by the Mafia because they will want to get their companions out of prison? It is ridiculous to think our jails are a deterrent; the prisoners live like they are in a hotel, and the word "lifelong" means, with good conduct, at the most twenty years in Switzerland. My own opinion is still wavering. On the one hand, giving tit for tat is for me, personally, disagreeable; on the other hand, is that person actually worthy to receive the benefit of my humane feeling?

ACTIVITY 5 Complete this analysis of the "Death Penalty" paragraph.

Controversial subject: _____

Reasons Against:

1. _____

2. _____

3. _____

Reasons For:

1. _____

2. _____

3. _____

EXPLANATION

The differences between a persuasive argument and a neutral argument is that in a neutral argument the writer is not attempting to persuade. In a neutral argument, the writer presents the information and lets the reader form his or her own conclusion. It is especially important in neutral argument to present information fairly and in a balanced way.

Paragraph 6   *Writing an Inductive Paragraph*

DIRECTIONS   *Write a paragraph in which you state some disturbing fact inductively.*

EMPTY DREAMS

Not long ago, a Japanese television reporter asked some Japanese children what their dreams were. One child answered, "My dream is to go to a good and very competitive school." Another child responded, "I want to be a businessman who makes a very good salary." These dreams might be considered reasonable for twenty-year-olds, or even for teenagers, but the two children questioned were six and seven years old, respectively. Somewhat later, in the same program, a five-year-old was asked what she dreamed of, and she answered quickly, "A personal computer." Do children no longer dream of wild and wonderful places full of magical and exotic creatures? Is there no room left for folktales, fairytales, myths, and legends? It is frighteningly clear that children's minds have more information than in the past, but is more information good for them? The world is becoming more realistic, and unless the children of this and future generations are encouraged to develop their imaginations, this realistic world will be inhabited by robots!

ACTIVITY 6 *Complete this analysis of the "Dreams" paragraph.*

Title: _____

Example 1: _____

Example 2: _____

Example 3: _____

Main idea: _____

_____

EXPLANATION

In an inductive paragraph, the writer begins by discussing the topic directly with examples, facts, or statistics. The topic sentence normally appears at the end of the paragraph.

Appendix A

Grammar Practice

Exercise 1   *Fragments*

DIRECTIONS   *Circle the number of each <u>incomplete sentence</u>.*

1. One of the most critical areas of the world, the Middle East.
2. Gandhi's assassination did not end his dream.
3. The nucleus, composed of electrons, protons, and neutrons.
4. Everywhere in northern Norway from Bodo to Narvik.
5. Research has shown that sharks are not colorblind.
6. The Chinese characters which form the basis of some Japanese characters.
7. Brasília, the capital of Brazil, is a new city.
8. Nowhere in the world is as dry as Chile's Atacama Desert.
9. Buddhism, Hinduism, and Islam have influenced the country's development.
10. Da Vinci, who painted the *Mona Lisa*, lived in Italy.
11. The French who colonized Algeria and have left their influence.
12. Not only the Indonesians but also the Malaysians.
13. Turkish and Finnish are closely related languages.
14. Ice cream sundaes, apple pies, and candy bars lack significant nutrition.
15. If you link Korean words.
16. The life expectancy of a man in Burkina Faso is only twenty-nine years.
17. For example, Singapore, Hong Kong, and Bangkok.
18. Nobody understands.
19. Especially in the United States and Canada.
20. Eucalyptus trees are well suited for dry climates.

Exercise 2   *Fragments*

DIRECTIONS   *Change each fragment into a complete sentence.*

a small piece broken

1. Both mathematics and biology.

_____

_____

2. Paris, a romantic city.

   Paris is a romantic city.

_____

3. Mao Tse-tung who wrote the *Red Book*.

   Mao Tse-tung is a familiar person. Who wrote
   the red book.

4. For instance, El Salvador, Nicaragua, and Honduras.

   For instance,   "   are in central
   America

5. If the weather is cold. 俟件.

   I wouldn't go out if the weather is cold.

_____

6. The Nile which is the longest river in the world.

   _____ " _____ *flows across africa*
   (moves)

7. From San Francisco to New York.

   ① From San Francisco to New York is a long
   distance ② what is the distance From San Francisco
   to New York

8. Because English is an international language.

   Everybody studies English because English
   is an international language.

9. At least some whales.

   At least some whales are in the habitat

_____

10. A high fever and an upset stomach.

   He gets a high fever and upset stomach

_____

Exercise 3   *Subject/Verb Agreement*

DIRECTIONS   *Find each sentence that has an error in agreement and correct it.*

1. Korea is one of the countries which has a problem with oil.

2. The analysis of the data was incorrect.

3. The president, with her husband, is improving our country.

4. Watson and Crick is famous for discovering DNA.

5. The California magpie is a beautiful bird that have a golden beak.

6. Neither roses nor tulips lives well in cold weather.

7. *Born in the USA* is one of Springsteen's best songs.

8. Algebra were invented by Arab mathematicians.

9. There are few people in the world who have had the impact of Buddha.

10. *Time* and *Newsweek* gives the reader a narrow view of world news.

11. Everyone are not visiting the Mediterranean this year.

12. The family are growing stronger again.

13. Colonial countries such as the United Kingdom inevitably lose power.

14. Coffee is a product whose price depends on the weather.

15. There are many species of organisms which thrives in Antarctica.

16. Not only does the Finns love to ski, but also they love to party.

17. The Lebanese people is in the midst of a national renewal.

18. Are there anything that tastes better than a hamburger and fries?

19. The Andes Mountains is home to a wide range of plant life.

20. Korean politics are very confusing.

Exercise 4   *Subject/Verb Agreement*

DIRECTIONS   *Complete each sentence using* is *or* are *as the verb.*

1. Either beer or wine _____

_____

2. French food _____

_____

3. The violin, like the cello, _____

_____

4. Intelligence _____

_____

5. *Manchete*, a famous Brazilian magazine throughout South America

_____

_____

6. The news from South Africa _____

_____

7. The Philippines _____

_____

8. The study of economics and philosophy _____

_____

9. Of all the countries in the world, the United States _____

_____

10. None of the policemen in town _____

_____

11. The Rolling Stones _____

_____

12. Many cups of coffee _____

_____

13. The planets in the solar system _____

_____

14. Physics _____

15. The newspaper, *The New York Times*, _____

_____

Exercise 5   *Articles*

DIRECTIONS   *Find each mistaken article and correct it. Add missing articles where needed. Some sentences may have more than one mistake; others, none.*

1. Trans-Siberian railroad crosses an entire Russia.

2. She kissed a man with a sunglasses on a right cheek.

3. Important subject for president and prime minister to discuss is population.

4. *Alien Resurrection* is violent movie in which many people are killed.

5. Babies should not drink cow's milk until they are at least a year old.

6. At top of mountain, a climbers stopped for the few minutes.

7. Poor people must always worry about where their next meal is coming from.

8. When the monsoon season comes, all of rice fields are flooded with water.

9. United Arab Emirates are located in a extremely important area of Arabian or Persian Gulf.

10. It is important for professors to enjoy teaching.

11. Serengeti Plain in the Kenya still has large herds of the wildebeest.

12. One of the easiest subjects to study is chemistry.

13. In the movie *Casablanca*, Bogart and Bergman are in love with each other.

14. Female students at universities always make higher grades than male students.

15. The king of the country made a new law forbidding alcohol.

16. Christianity and Judaism are two largest religions in United States.

17. Some of an animals are amphibious living on a land and in a sea.

18. Harvard University has the largest university library in the North America.

19. Fewer people are going to movies because they watch videos at home.

20. After five years of drought, Ethiopian farmers can produce no food.

Exercise 6   *Articles*

DIRECTIONS *Include the appropriate articles where necessary in the following sentences. In some blank spaces, no article is needed.*

1. After _____ long period of _____ time, some of _____ music will grow old.

2. At _____ University of _____ California, _____ school of veterinary medicine has _____ high reputation.

3. _____ Bering Strait separates _____ Russia from _____ United States.

4. During _____ month of _____ Ramadan, Muslims may not eat _____ food during _____ day.

5. *Don Quixote* is _____ interesting novel written in _____ 17th century by Cervantes.

6. Due to _____ heavy rains, _____ engineers could not build _____ new dam.

7. According to _____ most recent research, _____ AIDS is not transmitted by casual contact.

8. _____ only television in _____ Jordan is controlled by _____ government.

9. _____ dirt on _____ hillside on _____ side of _____ mountain on Oahu was washed away by heavy rain.

10. Even at _____ early age, _____ babies will smile at _____ adult's face.

11. _____ antique table in _____ hall is made of _____ cherry wood.

12. Many of _____ players on _____ basketball team admitted using _____ drugs.

13. _____ normal airplane ticket from _____ Los Angeles to _____ Shanghai costs _____ lot of money.

14. As _____ result of _____ war last year, thousands of refugees have left _____ country.

15. After _____ first storm of _____ season, workers always try to clear _____ roads.

Exercise 7   *Prepositions*

DIRECTIONS   *Choose the correct preposition for each blank.*

1. _____ top _____ the mountain is a large religious figure.

2. As the cat walked _____ the yard, it saw a bird _____ the tree.

3. _____ 1929 _____ 1940 there was a worldwide economic depression.

4. Because _____ the danger _____ infection, the children are not allowed _____ attend school.

5. The show that appeared _____ TV described the problems _____ minority groups _____ the United States.

6. John F. Kennedy was assassinated _____ November 22, 1963 _____ Lee Harvey Oswald.

7. The Red Sea is noted _____ its exotic fish; _____ least five hundred varieties can be seen _____ warm, clear waters.

8. The Singapore Embassy is located _____ Los Angeles _____ Wilshire Boulevard.

9. The theory _____ relativity and the discovery _____ the photoelectric effect are both attributed _____ Einstein.

10. When a young Japanese woman reaches the age _____ twenty-one, she is usually given a large party _____ her family.

11. The *Challenger* space shuttle probably crashed as a result _____ the failure _____ the rocket booster.

12. _____ the other hand, aspirin is effective _____ the reduction _____ clogged arteries.

13. Chinese tapestries made _____ silk are very valuable _____ the art world.

14. No visitor can ever forget the beautiful paintings _____ the Uffizi Galleries _____ Florence, Italy.

15. Krakatoa's eruption _____ the 1880s _____ the coast _____ Indonesia caused the largest explosion _____ recorded history.

Exercise 8   *Prepositions*

DIRECTIONS   *Choose the correct preposition for each blank.*

1. _____ 1970 _____ 1973, Salvador Allende was president _____ Chile.

2. Contrary _____ the popular image of serenity in outer space, there are a vast areas _____ incredible turmoil.

3. Chad has a population density _____ 9.32 per square mile, according _____ statistics released _____ 1998.

4. Gustave Thoeni _____ Italy won the world alpine skiing championship four times _____ the 1970s.

5. George Washington was born _____ February 22, 1732, _____ the state _____ Virginia.

6. The principle crops _____ the Central African Republic are cotton, coffee, and peanuts.

7. Many advertisers prefer radio _____ television because radio reaches a large segment _____ young people.

8. _____ the University _____ Missouri, there is an excellent department _____ sociology.

9. _____ the bottom _____ the leaf, many insects suck the juice.

10. Neanderthal man seems to have lived _____ Europe _____ around 200,000 years ago.

11. Located _____ the east coast _____ Africa, Djibouti is separated _____ the Arabian peninsula _____ the strait _____ of Bab el Mandeb.

12. Calcium, discovered _____ 1808 _____ Davy, has an atomic weight _____ 40.08.

13. Bears and pandas belong _____ the family _____ Ursidae.

14. Wilhelm Steinmetz _____ Austria was the first modern worldclass chess champion, retaining the title _____ 1866 _____ 1894.

15. One meter is equal _____ 39.37 inches.

Exercise 9   *Parallel Structure*

DIRECTIONS   *In each sentence find the unparallel element and correct it. Some sentences contain no mistake.*

1. The main differences are writing characters, pronunciation of vowels, and conjugating verbs.

2. Bolivia lost its oil-bearing area to Paraguay and its area of rubber to Brazil.

3. Having eaten and sleeping, the elephant seal finds a place on the beach.

4. The University of Alaska has 5,086 students and there are 400 teachers there too.

5. Pete Sampras won Wimbledon in 1998 and in the year 1997.

6. Two important contributors to Japanese physics were Shinichiro Tomonaga, who won the Nobel Prize in 1961, and Hideki Yukawa, a 1949 Nobel Prize winner.

7. To study languages, riding horses, and going to movies were his favorite activities.

8. Scientists can explain precisely how the memory works or about the spread of viruses.

9. The average American eats 144.5 pounds of beef, 50 pounds of canned vegetables, and fats and oils totaling 57 pounds per year.

10. Not only do the Himalayas have the highest mountain in the world but also they have the next twenty highest ones.

11. He believed that he could end the fighting and unite the people.

12. Lockheed Corporation, based in California, produces commercial aircraft and airplanes for the military.

13. The death penalty is imposed for adultery, raping a person, and terrorist activities.

14. Neither Australians nor people in Tasmania like kangaroos.

15. Both the *Pietà* in Rome and Florence's *David* are famous pieces of sculpture by Michelangelo.

Exercise 10   *Parallel Structure*

DIRECTIONS *In each sentence find the unparallel element and correct it.*

1. With curly hair and a bushy mustache, Mark Twain endeared himself to the American public through his novels and the way he looked.

2. How Mozart composed his music and the story of Mozart's life are the subject of *Amadeus*.

3. The test includes a section on gerunds, participles, and there is a part about infinitives.

4. Completely surrounded by South Africa, Lesotho must rely on her unfriendly neighbor for not only agricultural imports, but also exports of agricultural products.

5. Either the Iranian army or those soldiers who are fighting for Iraq must ultimately tire and lose the war.

6. Akiba learned that he would be executed and the Romans would expect him to renounce his God.

7. To be an effective president, one needs intelligence, an ability to decide, and humility.

8. The World Cup was won by Brazil in 1994 and by France in the year 1998.

9. Admired by fellow scientists and being distrusted, Robert Oppenheimer led the Manhattan Project, which produced the first atomic bomb.

10. To treat badly in school and family separation in cities are two of the main problems facing Kampuchea today.

11. Enjoying skiing as well as the opportunity to ride horses, Jackie Kennedy generated much enthusiasm in the sporting world.

12. Although the sale and consuming of drugs is illegal in Panama, there are many sellers willing to risk imprisonment.

13. Fearing for his life and because he sought a better life, Freud fled Austria in 1938.

14. Responding to the surge in domestic travel, TWA has decided that flights to Hawaii should be increased and less flights to Europe should be added.

15. From Morocco to Egypt, North Africa is an exciting blend of culture and traditional aspects.

Exercise 11   *Punctuation and Capitalization*

DIRECTIONS   *Add the appropriate punctuation and capitalization to the following paragraphs.*

because of his strong foreign policy richard nixon was a popular president in 1971 and 1972 in fact he was so popular that his opponent in the 1972 election george mcgovern of the democratic party had very little chance of defeating him however on june 17 1972 about four months before the election five men were arrested for breaking into the democratic national committee headquarters in washington d c at the time this arrest did not make news few people thought it was important on november 4 1972 richard nixon was reelected president by one of the largest margins in american history he won every state but one massachusetts

during 1973 and early 1974 the country became increasingly interested in the arrest which had taken place in 1972 the men who were arrested were sent to prison but they did not say whom they worked for at first president nixon said he had not ordered the break in nonetheless on june 25 1973 nixons lawyer john dean said that president nixon had tried to stop the police investigation of the break in around the end of july tape recordings were found which proved that nixon had known about the break in and had tried to stop the investigation on august 9 1974 richard nixon resigned the presidency the first and only president in american history ever to have done so

Exercise 12 *Punctuation and Capitalization*

DIRECTIONS *Add the appropriate punctuation and capitalization to the sentences below.*

1. after twenty years of rule ferdinand marcos left the philippines and moved to hawaii where he subsequently died

2. it is important to control your blood pressure so it wont control you

3. exceptional performance superb design and dependable quality are characteristic of goodrich tires

4. the $284000 three year research project found normal levels of cancer in residents of glen avon the community beside the toxic dump

5. according to *websters dictionary* silence can be defined as the absence of any sound or noise

6. gautama siddhartha the buddha lived in india from 563–483 bc

7. liechtenstein located between switzerland and austria has an area of only 65 square miles its population is a mere 11000

8. airport regulations require a minimum of 1200 feet visibility for planes to be allowed to land

9. macbeth othello and king lear are three tragedies written by shakespeare

10. the average chemist at the university of california davis makes $50000 a year

11. thomas a edison is famous for the quotation genius is one percent inspiration and ninety-nine percent perspiration

12. a typical 1999 dodge aspen station wagon with the usual accessories should cost about $20000

13. by the terms of the potsdam agreement silesia in the upper valley of the oder river was given to poland

14. after the money to operate the social security system runs out congress will have to appropriate additional funds

15. for example the 7 pm lecture at wellman hall is entitled nuclear energy in the united states

Exercise 13   *Punctuation and Capitalization*

DIRECTIONS   *Add the appropriate punctuation and capitalization to the paragraph.*

my favorite musical group is the style council because of the singers sexy nice voices and their songs the style council members are british musicians the lead singer belonged to the famous group jam before he formed the style council first when he sings his voice is wonderful a little husky and sexy for me the voices of the other group members complement the leaders voice very smoothly not only are their voices nice but also their songs are excellent their songs make me romantic because they dont have a strong sound and in some way they are old fashioned the type of sound that was popular in the 1940s 1950s the style councils music seems old fashioned but the music is not old the songs are skillfully arranged like modern music my favorite songs of theirs are youre the best thing and blue cafe when i listen to songs like these i feel as if im in a happy dream in conclusion the style council is a great group if you have a chance to listen to them youd better do so with your boyfriend or girlfriend

Exercise 14   *Wordiness*

DIRECTIONS   *Cross out all unnecessary words in the following sentences.*

1. The kangaroo can hop across the ground at a speed of almost 30 miles per hour.
2. Athens, the capital of Greece and the site of the Acropolis, suffers from heavy air pollution caused by cars.
3. A large, substantial portion of the world's copper is mined in Chile in South America.
4. The sparrow's wing which is used for flight contains an oily, water-resistant substance which helps keep the bird dry.
5. Rainbows are produced by the bending of light rays through water droplets in the sky.
6. Whales, inhabiting the world's oceans, are very social creatures which enjoy each other's company greatly.
7. There are numerous countries in the world which have the problem of overpopulation of people.
8. Unique among mammals, the platypus and echidna are the only ones which reproduce by laying eggs.
9. The paramount, most incredible example of man's inhumanity to man is Auschwitz.
10. The Ayatollah Khomeini caused fundamental, basic changes in Iranian society.
11. The pterodactyl, an old, ancient flying reptile, had no tail and used its beak for a rudder to fly with.
12. Mosquitoes love stagnant water because they like to deposit their eggs there.
13. Most of Darwin's research on evolution took place on his research expeditions to the Galápagos Islands.
14. Unlike grass, ivy can rapidly spread quickly over a large area of ground.
15. The South African economy is fueled by the sale of expensive materials such as gold, diamonds, and uranium which cost a lot of money.

Exercise 15   *Wordiness*

DIRECTIONS   *Rewrite this group of sentences as concisely as possible, removing unnecessary or obvious words, phrases, and clauses and combining sentences as appropriate.*

In the United States of America, a huge difference exists between the conditions of the rich and poor people. The country is very large, with fifty states, and has abundant raw materials and a lot of money. In fact, the United States is one of the richest countries in the world, and it has a lot of educated and intelligent people. So it should be easy for the United States to take care of all the people in the country. Still thousands of people have no homes, no money, and no food each day of their lives. I don't know exactly why it is like this. One reason may be that it's such a large country that it's hard to keep track of all the people in it. Moreover, the rich people with a lot of money don't need or want to give some of their money away to help the poorer people in the country.

Exercise 16   *Variety of Sentence Structure*

DIRECTIONS   *The following paragraph, while well written, lacks sentence variety. Notice that most of the sentences are in the following form: subject, verb, object. In the space on the following page, rewrite the italicized portions of the paragraph, varying the opening of each as indicated.*

Emily Dickinson, a poet in 19th-century America, is my favorite poet because I agree with her attitude toward society, and her irony strongly impresses me. [1]*The society didn't recognize that women were equal to men in those days.* [2]*Dickinson did not work for social change; she wrote her beliefs into her poetry.* I sometimes remember one of her poems entitled "Strawberry." [3]*A child in this poem wants a strawberry over the fence.* If she climbs on the fence she can get it. However, [4]*she will tear her dress and God will scold her.* [5]*So she only looks at the strawberry even though she knows she can reach it.* [6]*The child is surely Emily herself.* The strawberry represents freedom; God represents society. [7]*Dickinson's poems superficially describe beautiful, peaceful scenes, but always their true meaning is revealed through irony.* [8]*It is easy to sympathize with her poetry even though her poems were written one century ago.* After all, I cannot help considering that Japan is one century behind America as far as women's rights are concerned. [9]*My favorite poet will never change as long as I live in Japan.*

1. *(begin with prepositional phrase)* _____

_____

_____

2. *(begin with participial phrase)* _____

_____

_____

3. *(begin with prepositional phrase)* _____

_____

_____

4. *(make the first clause passive)* _____

_____

_____

5. *(begin with adverb clause)* _____

_____

_____

6. *(begin with single adverb)* _____

_____

_____

7. *(begin with single adverb)* _____

_____

_____

8. *(begin with an infinitive phrase)* _____

_____

_____

9. *(begin with adverb clause)* _____

_____

_____

Exercise 17   *Variety of Sentence Structure*

DIRECTIONS   *In the space on the following page, rewrite the italicized portions of the paragraph, varying the structure as indicated.*

[1]*Sweden is the greatest country in the world to live in because it has political democracy, social safety, and religious freedom.* In Sweden [2]*the government treats the people* with political respect. [3]*In fact, the political democracy is complete. It doesn't make any difference if a person is a communist or a conservative.* Second, the government allows everyone to benefit from the social safety system. [4]*This system is paid for by one of the highest tax rates in the world.* But what difference does it make? After all, it is possible to go to a dentist for two dollars and to go to a doctor for five dollars. [5]*For each person under sixteen years of age, dental and medical services are free!* Third, no Swede has to be a member of the state Protestant church. [6]*Some people are members, and others are not.* Everybody may, if she oɪ he desires, join an Indian religion such as Buddhism or praise Allah. The choice is free. In summary, freedom in Sweden is based on respect and understanding for other people, not on money or status. This fact makes Sweden the best country to live in!

1. (*make into a simple sentence; begin with:* "Sweden's political democracy . . .") _____

   _____

   _____

2. (*make passive; delete subject*) _____

   _____

   _____

3. (*combine sentences,* "so . . . that") _____

   _____

   _____

4. (*reduce to an adjective clause and combine with preceding sentence*)

   _____

   _____

   _____

5. (*change to conditional,* "if . . . then") _____

   _____

   _____

6. (*change to a complex sentence,* "even though") _____

   _____

   _____

Exercise 18   *Transition Words*

DIRECTIONS   *Use the following transition words to complete this paragraph:*

finally   for example   moreover   however   nonetheless   indeed

Because of its art and its new conception of man, the Renaissance is the most enticing Western historical period that can be imagined. Surprisingly and ironically, "Renaissance" starts with the prefix "re-" meaning "again;" _____ , the idea of simple imitation of what had been done before never occurred to the artists, writers, or scientists of the Renaissance.

_____ , every new project was undertaken following a lucid principle: "Greek and Roman civilizations were the best; _____ , we are capable of surpassing their achievements overwhelmingly." _____ , Raphael, Michelangelo, and Cortona were but a few of the many remarkable artists of the time. _____ , who in the history of Western art has been able to surpass the perfection of St. Peter's, Leonardo's madonnas, Botticelli's indescribable drawings, or Giambologna's dazzling statues? _____ , confidence in the new image of man, a man closer to the Divinity, almost a god, emerged from the terrible grave of the Middle Ages. Nature was startlingly controlled; science began to bear fruit. Man as God's rival and nature's sovereign: Who before or after has dared so much?

When you finish each writing assignment, evaluate your own work on a copy of the following checklist. Then submit the evaluation to your teacher with your paragraph.

	+ excellent	✔ average	— poor

	Self-evaluation	Teacher's evaluation

Does the paragraph have:

Elements and organization

	Self-evaluation	Teacher's evaluation
1. a clear title?	_____	_____
2. a complete topic sentence?	_____	_____
3. appropriate order?	_____	_____
4. appropriate transitions?	_____	_____
5. a strong summary sentence?	_____	_____

Form

6. continuous form?	_____	_____
7. appropriate punctuation?	_____	_____
8. accurate capitalization?	_____	_____
9. correct spelling?	_____	_____
10. clear handwriting?	_____	_____

Grammar

11. no run-on sentences/fragments?	_____	_____
12. subject/verb agreement?	_____	_____
13. correct verb tenses?	_____	_____
14. correct articles/prepositions?	_____	_____
15. other? (*Teacher only*)	_____	_____

Content and style

16. originality?	_____	_____
17. deep ideas?	_____	_____
18. complete development?	_____	_____
19. varied sentence structure?	_____	_____

Teacher's general comments _____

_____

_____